THE COMPLETE
Crafty
COOK BOOK

MICHAEL BARRY

THE COMPLETE
Crafty
COOK BOOK

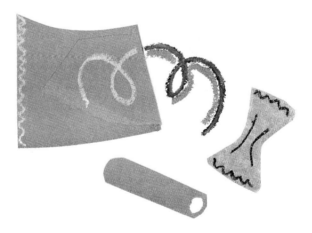

<u>Collins</u>

8 Grafton Street, London
1988

William Collins Sons and Co Ltd
London · Glasgow · Sydney · Auckland
Toronto · Johannesburg ·

First published in Great Britain 1988

Executive Editor: Louise Haines

Design: Janet James
Photographs: Andrew Whittuck
Food preparation: Berit Vinegrad
Styling: Bobby Baker
Illustrations: Sarah McMenemy

BRITISH LIBRARY CATALOGUING IN PUBLICATION DATA
Barry, Michael
The Complete Crafty Cook Book
1. Cookery, International
1 Title
641.5   TX725.A1

ISBN 0 00 411225 3

Filmset in Plantin Light
by Qualitext Typesetting, Abingdon

Made and printed in Great Britain
Hartnolls Ltd, Bodmin, Cornwall.

Contents

Dedication

For my mother who taught me my cooking
and for my wife who cheerfully puts up with it.

Introduction

Crafty cooking is all Michael Aspel's fault really. It was on his show on Capital Radio in London that the name and the idea first appeared. I was once asked to stand in for his cookery broadcaster and, in a bit of a panic, decided to do some of the easiest food I knew. That first menu is printed on page 11 in all its horror and glory, but there is a story behind it.

For years I had been cooking by a method that I thought of as the lazy way to cook. It basically meant taking a recipe that I liked and seeing how many stages I could leave out before you could tell the difference in the taste or the texture. What usually surprised me was that you could often leave out plenty and all you missed was the hard work. A couple of weeks of these labour-saving techniques convinced Mr Aspel that he was in on the birth of one of the great revolutions in British gastronomy. 'I know what you're up to,' he announced one day, 'you're just doing crafty cooking, with the hard parts left out.'

He was, of course, right, and once I had realised what it was I was really doing there was no holding me. I simplified and adapted everything in sight. The results were sometimes great and, just occasionally, terrible! But the underlying aim, to make good and delicious food easier to cook, less frightening and more achievable, remained the same. And the same it's stayed despite changes in taste, ingredients and knowledge.

At the very time this incredible (and edible) discovery was going on, a whole range of new foods was appearing throughout the country. Thanks to people like Elizabeth David and Robert Carrier, the interest in cooking was extending into new areas and new worlds at the same time. Some people, myself included, were cooking for fun as well as necessity, and the exotic scents of Provence and the Orient, of Mexico and Morocco, were abroad in the land. It's a process that is continuing today, even faster now that good food and cookery has become a popular hobby and also big business. But fourteen years ago it was a bit different, it was just beginning. The whole idea of unusual foods was surprising to many, and there were mistakes as well as successes. But what became clear over the next few years was that there were a number of techniques as well as recipes that could be 'craftified'. Some of them were simply a fresh approach, like the crafty White Sauce (see page 23), some were based on new equipment such as the blender or the food processors that have followed it, like the potted meats (see page 58).

Since that first radio menu there have been over a thousand broadcasts, five books, many articles, demonstrations and teaching sessions. In all of these areas I have had the privilege of learning and listening as well as talking and showing. The public taste has changed and become far more informed and sophisticated – for the better in a big way. Healthy eating has become an important part of all our lives, and my tastes and 'craftifications' have changed at the same time. I'm not any thinner to prove it, but concern for what goes into our food as well as what food goes into us, has become second nature.

This book then is a selection from the thousands of recipes and ideas that have made up crafty cooking so far. They are my favourites and I hope some of yours too. While they include some of the early crafties, most are from more recent times when ingredients, enthusiasm and ideas have been at their freshest.

One important thought before we begin: real crafty cooking is not a series of techniques or even of recipes. It's an attitude of mind that says food is fun, it's about pleasure, love, taste and sharing. It's meant to be enjoyed whether you are cooking or eating it. I hope this book is the basis for your own dishes, variations and craftiness. And I hope you enjoy them and the results with friends and those you love as much as I have.

Michael Barry
SUMMER 1988

The First Crafty Menu
Spring 1974

———

SERVES 4
LOBSTER IN SHRIMP SOUP
HOT FRENCH BREAD

———

HERBED RACK OF LAMB
CLEMENT FREUD'S POTATOES AND
GREEN BEANS

———

ICED CHERRIES
COFFEE

Lobster in Shrimp Soup

1 can Lobster Bisque
1 small carton single cream
1 tablespoon sherry
50g (2 oz) peeled shrimps

Mix together the soup and cream and heat (do not boil). Just before serving, add the sherry and shrimps and serve with hot French bread, which has been warmed in the oven for 10 minutes and buttered.

Herbed Rack of Lamb

1 rack best end of lamb (8 chops)
1 dessertspoon mustard (any kind)
Garlic salt
Dried rosemary
1 tablespoon redcurrant jelly

Ask the butcher to chine and skin the lamb. (Do not let him chop it!) At home, trim 2.5cm (1 inch) of meat off the bone – it is not essential, but looks more attractive. Place on a rack in a roasting pan and spread with the mustard. Sprinkle with the garlic salt and rosemary if you have it. Add a glass of water to the pan. Roast in a preheated oven at approximately 180°C (350°F) gas mark 4, for 40 minutes. To make the gravy, mix the redcurrant jelly with the juices in the pan.

Clement Freud's Potatoes and Green Beans

750g (1½ lb) potatoes
750g (1½ lb) green beans (stringless)

Wash the potatoes but do not peel them – boil, drain and butter. Top and tail stringless beans – crafty cooks do not buy runner beans – and boil them until they are cooked, but still bright green.

Iced Cherries

500g (1 lb) of the darkest cherries you can find

Pick them over and leave on the stalks. Place them in your prettiest bowl, cover with water and add some ice cubes. Serve them with a saucer of caster sugar for each guest to dip their cherries in.

	Cost
Soup and bread	70
Lamb and vegetables	1.15
Cherries	40
Total cost	£2.25

Crafty cook musts Coffee Bags
Suggested wine Light Red

The Crafty Kitchen Cupboard

Here are a few thoughts on the contents of a crafty kitchen. Ingredients are the key to crafty cooking, so I've suggested a useful storecupboard and fridge list to help you on your way. There's also a list of crafty kitchen items that my years of slaving over hot stoves have led me to prize. I've also included some thoughts on choosing and keeping fresh food. The lists are not meant to be comprehensive and I haven't used brand names except when they really matter.

Cooking Equipment

Storecupboard
Cans

Tomatoes – Italian, peeled, chopped, pasatta
Tuna – in brine and oil
Anchovies – in oil
Sardines – in olive oil if possible
Mangoes or mango purée

Bottles

Sauces:
Heinz Tomato – no additives at all
Kikkoman's Soy – the best there is
Langans' Chili – the best there is

Miscellaneous:
Dijon mustard ⎫
Grain mustard ⎬ French

Sunflower oil
Olive oil
Sweet mango chutney
Mint jelly – home-made if possible
Apricot jam – home-made if possible
Marmalade – home-made if possible
Tiptree Strawberry Jam

Flours

Wholemeal
Strong white
White cake flour (plain and self-raising)
Cornflour
Arrowroot
Oatmeal (fine and coarse)

Rice

Basmati (for savouries)
Pudding

Pulses

White haricot beans
Green flageolet beans
Red kidney beans
Chick peas
Red lentils

Pastas

White and green tagliatelle
Pasta shells or bows
Lasagne sheets
Chinese noodles

Spices and Dried Herbs

Fresh herbs are nicest when you can get them, though dried ones are fine if you can't and often give a very intense flavour. I sometimes use dried herbs in preference to fresh in winter stews and casseroles because of this intensity. However, parsley and basil, which can be bought dried, never taste the same.

Coriander
Cumin
Chili powder
Turmeric
Mustard powder
White and black peppercorns
Cinnamon
Cloves
Nutmeg
Allspice
Cardamom
Paprika
Garam masala
Garlic salt
Celery salt

Sea salt – Malden is the best
Chives
Mint
Parsley
Dill
Celery seed
Rosemary
Thyme
Sage
Oregano
Marjoram
Tarragon
Bay leaves (whole and powdered)
Garlic cloves

The Fearless Fridge Fillers

1 carton thick double cream (with re-usable top)
1 jar grated Parmesan cheese
1 jar mayonnaise (home-made [see page 27] or Hellmans')
1 large carton natural yoghurt (Greek-style)
1 jar fromage frais
1 jar black olives/kalamata
1 jar capers
1 jar green peppercorns
1 jar tomato purée
25g (8 oz) Gruyère cheese
1 bottle walnut oil (for salad dressings)
1 bottle lemon juice (the cloudy kind)

Fresh Food Shopping

The following books are available to guide you to the best suppliers in your area:

British Food Finds 1987 by Henrietta Green
Directory of Fine Food by Simone Sekers (Hodder & Stoughton)
Guide to Good Food Shops by Susan Campbell (Macmillan)

Meat

Don't buy from a supermarket if you can help it. Buy from a butcher who doesn't use an electric saw to cut the meat, and who hangs beef or lamb (to tenderise and mature them) and other meats for their proper length of time. Bright redness is *not* a sign of freshness – it can be a sign of toughness. Find a good expert and take advice. There are a number of suppliers of meat that has been raised without growth hormones or other additives – see the books above.

Fish

Fresh fish glistens and the eyes are not shrunken and dry. Find a supplier who will fillet, skin and give you the bits for soup. Always start with a whole fish if you can. Always demand smoked fish *without* any extra colour – it's better for you and means you can see what you're buying.

Vegetables

Organic vegetables are widely available and worth the extra money for their flavour – especially root vegetables (and, in the case of fruit, lemons which have no wax on their skins). Otherwise, buy often and ready to eat; vegetables picked so long ago as not to be ripe when *you* buy them will lack flavour and sweetness. Look for the new taste-orientated varieties in some shops.

CRAFTY TIP

If you have to buy unripe avocados, melons or mangoes, put them in a paper bag in a dry, warm drawer to ripen. That way they don't go bitter or rotten so easily.

Fruit

Buy ripe and, when you can, in season – strawberries in the summer, apples in the autumn – they are cheaper, fresher and will taste better. Again, look for the taste-orientated varieties coming into the shops, particularly in things like English apples. Tropical fruit like avocados, melons and mangoes should be bought ripe and are best eaten simply. Supermarkets that specialise in them have good explanatory leaflets available. All ripe fruit keeps best in the fridge and, in or out of the fridge, in a basket or dish where the air can circulate.

Eggs and Poultry

Always buy free-range or corn-raised chickens and eggs if you can find them – apart from the humanitarian aspect, they taste better and are better for you! All ducks and turkeys are essentially 'free-range' by their nature.

Milk and Cheeses

Low-fat milks and cheeses are widely available now and very good some are too, both for health and flavour.

Semi-skimmed milk is best for cooking and tea – skimmed does lack flavour and body. Look for unpasteurised milk and, if you are vegetarian, non-animal rennet. Plain yoghurt, especially the strained Greek kind, and fromage frais – very creamy but low in fat – keep well in the fridge and are always worth having.

Do look out for the great range of British cheeses made on farms and smallholdings all over the country and, once again, there is a book, *The Great British Cheese Book* by Patrick Rance (Macmillan), to help. New or revived flavours are coming up every month, soft and hard, cows' milk, goats' and sheep's milk cheeses.

Bread

Real bread (try to find a small local baker who knows the difference) keeps well in a plastic bag for two days or so. It also freezes surprisingly well. I often keep a packet of German-made Volk Brot, sealed in its wrappings, in the larder. It lasts six months and is a great emergency standby.

CRAFTY TIP

To revive bread, especially French bread or rolls that are stale, rinse quickly under a cold tap, put in a brown paper bag and place in a preheated oven 180°C (350°F) gas mark 4, for 10 minutes – eat while warm.

Kitchen Equipment

This is not intended to be a comprehensive guide to kitchen planning; I'm just identifying those things that I find help make cooking crafty.

Knives

These must be sharp and sharpenable when they have been blunted by use. They should, despite conventional wisdom about carbon steel, be stainless for convenience, and have solid riveted handles. I find the Smithfield or French- or German-made Sabatier-type knives the best and most easily sharpened, though the Japanese have just introduced a wonderful new range in a similar style. You need one 10 –13cm (4 –5 inch) knife and one 20 –25cm (8–10 inch) knife. An intermediate size and a chopper are useful additions, as is a serrated knife for fruit and so forth.

Saucepans

Aim for stainless steel with an aluminium sandwich bottom, or heavy-duty aluminium with or without a top quality nonstick coating. The key is to have heavy gauge metal, strong safe handles and lids you can take off when they're hot – don't laugh, I've seen prize-winning designs which you have needed a knife to prise open when heated. A small top-class *nonstick* pan is a great boon for milk or jam heating, so is a deep frying pan with a lid for many uses.

Casseroles

I like enamelled cast iron in a range of sizes, but I also have a couple of earthenware pots that go back a quarter of a century and are fabulous for bean dishes and really slow cooking. Look out for a new steam sealed casserole (*not* a pressure cooker) I helped to develop which bakes, casseroles and braises wonderfully with a great benefit in flavour from the seal. It's called a Cataplana Marie.

Food Processors

These are a must for crafty cooks. There are many on the market, most of them good. I've used the same one for twelve years (a cheap ordinary one) and wouldn't be without it. The hand held ones are all right, but a table model with a good sized bowl and a range of graters, slicers and so on is better. You shouldn't need a blender or food mixer as well.

Gadgets

Everyone has their favourites. There are very few that I couldn't be without but *they* are crafty and important to me:

Egg beater whisk.   I use the kind that looks like a bedspring wrapped around a coat hanger hook. It will beat anything in no time at all and has saved many a sauce from lumpy destruction.

Potato/vegetable/fruit peeler.   This has a simple sharpening motion and thinly peels anything that's peelable – cheap and indispensable.

Lemon zester.   All the flavour and no pith with this little unlikely-looking tool – never grate a lemon again (or an orange or grapefruit).

Apple cutter. This cores and separates apples or pears in a single stroke – giving pretty results and effortless working. It was the great success (totally accidentally) of the first Food and Drink series I worked on.

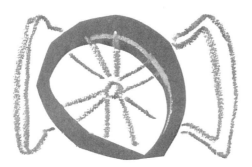

Other equipment

Plenty of wooden spoons; a plastic spatula for scraping basins, saucepans and processor bowls; good sieves; can openers; colanders; a ladle; plenty of assorted bowls and gratin dishes; and a large, stable chopping board are the other things that distinguish a crafty kitchen – or at least mine.

Crafty Sauces

There are just five key sauces that make up the crafty repertoire. All five are basic, internationally known and loved sauces that have a huge number of variations and additions. They will make almost all the special sauces you will ever need as a crafty cook. I've developed, borrowed and adapted these classic recipes over the years and the following sauces are foolproof, easy, and indistinguishable from the 'real' thing.

They need very little time to make (though the Tomato Sauce benefits from twenty minutes' to half-an-hour's simmering) and the only special equipment you will need is a food processor or blender. (They can be made by hand if you prefer, but that isn't really crafty cooking so I've put in the processor recipes.) The White Sauce dates from my early Capital Radio days before the advent of food processors . . . . there, that dates me!

If the techniques seem a little strange or even chancey to you – and they're likely to if you haven't been brought up crafty – try the recipe before you need it. Not only will it give you confidence that there may be method in my madness, but it's also a chance to experiment with some of the suggested variations in small but delicious quantities.

White Sauce (Béchamel)

This uses a totally different technique from the one that's been taught for years. It seems to have emerged only about ten years ago, and depends on the use of a special whisk that I first described on the radio as looking like a coathanger with a bedspring wrapped around it! It's still the best description, as you can see from the illustration on page 20. You could use any kind of whisk but it won't work so well.

The type of flour you use depends on the dish – the more robust sauces need plain flour, the lighter kind do very well with cornflour. More flour makes a thicker sauce, more liquid makes a runnier one. The key thing is to remember to WHISK WELL! If you do, it only takes about two minutes from a very unpromising looking beginning to a smooth, shiny sauce.

MAKES 300ML (½ PINT)
300ml (½ pint) milk (full cream or semi-skimmed)
1 tablespoon flour
1 tablespoon butter (only butter has the flavour)
Pinch each of powdered bay leaves and salt

Put the milk in a heavy-based pan, preferably a nonstick one. Whisk in the flour, then add the other ingredients. Whisk again and bring gently to the boil, whisking regularly. When the sauce thickens, give it a really good stir and simmer for 1 minute. That's all there is to it – it's ready to use.

VARIATIONS

The variations are, like those of any white sauce, almost endless. The secret is to make the sauce smoothly first, *then* add the other ingredients.

Cheese Sauce (Mornay)

2 tablespoons grated cheese (Gruyère is nice, so is Cheddar or
*   Lancashire)*
1 teaspoon made mustard

Parsley Sauce

4 tablespoons chopped parsley
1 dessertspoon lemon juice

Onion Sauce

250g (8 oz) onion, chopped and sautéed for 10 minutes
*   in 2 tablespoons butter*
½ teaspoon grated nutmeg

Mustard Sauce

2 tablespoons Dijon or grain mustard
1 teaspoon caster sugar

Hollandaise Sauce

Despite its Dutch name, this is a French sauce. Traditionally it takes twenty minutes and total concentration to make. However, with a food processor or blender it takes only two minutes from scratch. It has an incomparably delicate flavour that is delicious with fish, particularly poached salmon, and light dishes, especially chicken. Try it on simply boiled new potatoes, too – superb.

MAKES ABOUT 200ML (⅓ PINT)
125g (4 oz) unsalted or lightly salted butter
1 egg plus 1 egg yolk
1 teaspoon lemon juice
Salt and white pepper

Cut the butter into chunks and melt it in a small saucepan until it foams but does not turn brown. Place the egg, egg yolk, lemon juice, a pinch of salt and pepper in a blender or food processor and process for 5 seconds. Then, with the motor running, carefully pour the foaming butter in through the feed tube. Process for 3 seconds until smooth.

Tip the mixture into the saucepan and reheat over a low heat, or in a double boiler, until it suddenly thickens (30 seconds). Stop cooking it at this point or it will become fancy scrambled eggs!

It can be kept warm for up to 10 minutes without any major harm coming to it, but should be eaten quickly and as fresh as possible.

Sauce Béarnaise

This is *the* French sauce for red meats. It's supposed to have been James Bond's favourite with steak. Certainly the double fillet, Châteaubriand with Sauce Béarnaise is one of the classic dishes of *haute cuisine*. But if you're feeling the pinch a bit towards the end of the week, it's quite nice with hamburgers, too! It's amazing what a transformation a little special touch can make to an everyday family meal.

MAKES ABOUT 200ML (⅓ PINT)
1 small onion or shallot, very finely chopped
2 tablespoons wine or tarragon vinegar
1 egg plus 1 egg yolk
½ teaspoon real French mustard
125g (4 oz) unsalted or lightly salted butter

Place the onion or shallot and vinegar in a small saucepan, bring to the boil and cook until the vinegar is reduced by half.

Place the egg, egg yolk and mustard in a food processor or blender and process for 3 seconds.

Melt the butter in a separate saucepan until foaming but not brown then, with the motor running, pour it into the egg mixture. Process for 3 or 4 seconds until smooth, then add to the onion and vinegar reduction. Stir until blended, then heat gently until the mixture thickens – stop immediately.

Like Hollandaise, this sauce shouldn't be kept waiting much more than 10 minutes.

Tomato Sauce

This is the basic sauce of southern Europe, as white sauce is of northern. Oil based, it is at its best when given a chance to amalgamate its flavours by a twenty to thirty minute simmering. In the gloriously warm south, the heart of the sauce, red, ripe tomatoes, are literally to be found on every street corner. I'm afraid that their unique qualities of richness and red lusciousness simply do not exist in our anaemic versions or the warehouse-ripened imports we get. The only satisfactory substitute used to come in cans from Italy, and the canned plum tomatoes are still fine for the recipe. But now, thanks to the new technology of Tetra-packs, there is an alternative. It's called pasatta and is a sieved and thickened purée of the same Mediterranean tomatoes, with nothing added but a pinch of salt.

The variations of the sauce really rely on adding or subtracting flavours: garlic used mildly or in profusion; lemon juice or rind, or both; orange zest to provide a sparkle; anchovies to give bite; herbs for extra taste. My favourites among these are basil with its wonderful affinity with tomatoes, oregano for the true Italian 'pizazz', or coriander and chili for a North African flavour.

MAKES ABOUT 600ML (1 PINT)
2 tablespoons olive or peanut oil
250g (8 oz) onions, sliced
1 clove of garlic, chopped
500ml (18 fl oz) pasatta (or 500g [1 lb] can tomatoes)
1 tablespoon tomato purée
½ teaspoon each salt and sugar

Heat the oil in a pan and sauté the onions and garlic for 2 minutes, without browning. Add the pasatta or tomatoes and simmer for 2 minutes, then stir in the other ingredients. Part-cover and leave to simmer on the lowest heat possible for at least 10 minutes; 20–30 minutes is best to get all the richness this sauce is capable of.

Add any extra flavours, except fresh herbs, at the start of the simmering; add fresh herbs at the end for maximum impact.

Mayonnaise

This classic cold sauce is said to have been invented in honour of one of Napoleon's victories, but its history goes back a lot further than the early nineteenth century. It is traditionally one of the most difficult sauces of all to make, requiring great skill to add the oil drop by drop. Now, thanks to electricity, it's one of the easiest and quickest to make. Have courage and try it! If it does go wrong and curdle, by some accident or mistake, simply pour it out of the food processor or blender, add another egg to the machine, then add the curdled mixture in the same way as the oil in the recipe below – you'll just have twice as much mayonnaise at the end, that's all.

Double the quantities if you wish – you may have to if you own one of the big capacity processors – as this mayonnaise, which has a lovely light lemony flavour, will keep perfectly for a week in the refrigerator, if well covered.

You can make mayonnaise by hand but using only egg yolks, three of them, and not the egg whites. It's much thicker and heavier – and not very crafty.

MAKES ABOUT 300ML (½ PINT)

1 egg
½ teaspoon salt
½ teaspoon granulated sugar
2 teaspoons lemon juice
½ teaspoon made French mustard
250ml (8 fl oz) salad oil – mix in a little olive oil for a true
   French flavour

Put the egg, salt, sugar, lemon juice and mustard in a food processor or blender and process for 10 seconds. Add a quarter of the oil and process for 5 seconds. Remove the cover and, with the motor running, gradually pour in the rest of the oil in a slow, steady stream. The sound of the motor will suddenly change as the mayonnaise thickens, but just go on adding the oil and let the mayonnaise get thicker.

VARIATION

Green Mayonnaise (Sauce Verte)

Place a generous handful of herbs, for example parsley, young spinach leaves, chives or a little sorrel in a food processor and process for 10 seconds. Remove from the bowl and set aside.

Make the mayonnaise as on page 27. Once it has thickened, stop the motor and add the chopped herbs. Switch on again, add a little more oil and process for a few seconds to blend.

This is also a delicious accompaniment to cold beef or tongue.

Lemonette Salad Dressing

This is the crafty recipe for what's known as vinaigrette or French dressing. It has a flavour combination that comes from the Middle East where they eat an enormous variety and range of salads. The lemon juice makes it lighter than vinegar in similar recipes and has the other great advantage of not destroying the flavour of the food you are eating. It can be made with a whisk, but a food processor or blender makes it extra thick.

MAKES ABOUT 450ML (¾ PINT)

60ml (2 fl oz) lemon juice (fresh if possible, though bottled is fine)
½ teaspoon mustard powder
½ teaspoon salt
1 scant teaspoon sugar
120ml (4 fl oz) salad oil

Put all the ingredients, except the oil, in a food processor or blender and process for 3 to 5 seconds. With the motor running, pour in the oil in a steady stream. The dressing will thicken quite dramatically to a lovely single-cream consistency. It will coat each lettuce leaf or cling to the cucumber.

VARIATION

This garlic and herb variation is becoming increasingly popular abroad, but is very rarely tried here. It's not a taste for people who don't like garlic, or who aren't well acquainted with each other, but for those who do and are, it's almost good enough to eat on its own with hot crusty French bread.

Finely chop 2 quartered cloves of garlic and a handful of fresh herbs. Add the lemon juice and seasonings and proceed as above.

Soup for Supper

'Soup of the evening, beautiful Soup!' Sentiments from Lewis Carroll that I share completely: Cold Apple Soup on a hot summer's day; bubbling Gratin of Onion Soup to warm you after a brisk winter's walk; elegant Creamy Spinach Soup to begin the perfect dinner party. Soups are among crafty life's greatest pleasures. But for too many of us, and for too long, soup has simply meant something out of a can or packet. This is surely madness when home-made soup in endless varieties is cheap, quick and so little trouble. Our problem is that we haven't yet got into the habit shared by the French, the Italians and the Chinese of regarding a meal, let alone a day, without soup as incomplete.

Soup has been a part of crafty cooking from the beginning. In the days before the birth of the food processor or even the widespread use of the blender, I spent some time trying to find ways of making smooth soups without endless sieving by hand. This, on one occasion, included the use of cans of pease pudding! Such desperate expedients should be behind us now, but I think and hope that the sheer convenience and flavour of these soups will make you want to try your hand. These are just some of my favourites – I hope they will encourage you to soup up some of your own.

Greek Lemon Soup

This is a version of *Avgolémono*, the Greek combination of eggs, stock and lemons used as a sauce or even a dressing. I used to say stock cubes would do, but not any more I'm afraid. Use the bones from a chicken with herbs and onion to make your own stock – it's well worth the trouble.

SERVES 4–6
900ml (1½ pints) chicken stock (see page 97)
1 lemon
2 eggs
350g (12 oz) button mushrooms, thinly sliced
Salt and freshly ground black pepper

Heat the stock until boiling, then take it off the heat and let it cool for a minute or so. Squeeze the lemon into a small bowl and beat in the eggs. Add a ladleful of the stock and mix well. Pour the lemon and egg mixture into the saucepan containing the stock and whisk the whole lot together until smooth. Heat until it has almost boiled – don't let it actually boil though. The soup will thicken to about the consistency of single cream. Take it off the heat, add the mushrooms, and season to taste.

CRAFTY TIP

If disaster strikes when entertaining, don't panic! If you've over-cooked the vegetables, simply purée them with butter or cream and serve. If you've been over-generous with the seasoning in a soup or casserole, simply stir in a little yoghurt.

Vichyssoise

This cold soup, made of very ordinary ingredients like leeks and potatoes, is one of the great dishes in restaurants around the world. It's supposed to have been developed in America, when a French chef, who'd made it as a hot soup, was kept waiting so long by an insensitive guest that he let the soup get cold and added the cream as a guilty last-minute thought. Whether that story is true or not, it's certainly worth your while trying it without any guilt whatsoever. Don't use any butter though, it makes the soup go grainy!

SERVES 4–6

750g (1½ lb) leeks
2 tablespoons oil
750g (1½ lb) potatoes, cut into 2.5cm (1 inch) cubes
1 onion, cut into 2.5cm (1 inch) cubes
900ml (1½ pints) chicken stock (see page 97)
125ml (4 fl oz) double cream
Salt and freshly ground black pepper
Chopped chives to garnish

Peel any broken leaves off the leeks. Slice them in half lengthways and leave in cold water for at least 10 minutes before washing thoroughly to clear out all the dirt. Cut into 2.5cm (1 inch) lengths.

Heat the oil in a large pan and fry all the vegetables gently until softened. Add a good pinch of salt and pepper, cover with the stock and simmer for 30 minutes; the vegetables should be completely soft but not disintegrated.

Place all the vegetables in a food processor or blender, with enough stock to let the blades work. Process until the vegetables are completely smooth, adding a little more stock if necessary. Return the mixture to the remaining stock in the saucepan and stir until completely smooth. Pour into a bowl and chill in the refrigerator for at least 2 hours, until thoroughly cold.

To serve, ladle the soup into individual bowls, swirl the cream around the top so it forms a spiral and sprinkle the top of the soup with chives. (If fresh chives aren't available, use the freeze-dried version instead.) Serve with hot French bread.

Vichy Soup

No relation to Vichyssoise, the lovely golden colour of this carrot soup makes it extremely appetising, especially on a cold winter's day. The yoghurt is not traditional, but rather a modern, crafty touch; try it, it cuts the sweetness of the carrots just perfectly for my taste. The soup is named after the area of France famous for its cooking of carrots.

SERVES 4–6

1–2 tablespoons oil
750g (1½ lb) carrots, cut into chunks
2 potatoes, cut into chunks
2 onions, cut into chunks
½ teaspoon turmeric
900ml (1½ pints) chicken stock (see page 97)
1 carton natural yoghurt
Salt and freshly ground black pepper

Heat the oil in a deep saucepan, add all the vegetables and toss well, to prevent them sticking. Sprinkle with the turmeric and turn them until thoroughly coated. Add the stock, bring to the boil, then cover and simmer for 25 minutes.

Place all the vegetables in a food processor or blender with enough stock (about a third) to make a purée. Process for 15 seconds. Return the mixture to the stock in the saucepan, season to taste and heat through. Pour into a tureen.

Beat the yoghurt until smooth and slightly runny, then stir into the soup so that it swirls into a marble pattern.

VARIATION

In eastern Europe they sometimes make a similar soup to this with a few caraway seeds added at the initial frying stage. They make an interesting and unusual alternative flavour, as does a piece of star anise, available from Chinese groceries.

Soupe de Poisson

A universal soup, widely ignored in England for some reason. My version has ancestors from both Scotland and the Mediterranean, where they share a liking for rich-flavoured soups made with the produce of the sea. This recipe is extremely economical, as any good fishmonger should let you have (when you're buying something else, of course) a couple of good fish heads, preferably cod, halibut or turbot. You can use specially bought fish, but there's actually more flavour in the head. Don't let the eyes put you off!

SERVES 4

*2 large fish heads or 750g (1 1/2 lb) assorted fish trimmings – bones are
    fine!*
1 bay leaf
1 bunch of parsley
3 tablespoons lemon juice
1 clove of garlic, quartered
1 large onion, quartered
1 small can tomatoes or pasatta
Salt and freshly ground black pepper

Wash the fish heads or fish, place in a large saucepan and cover generously with water – the amount depends on the size of the heads and the saucepan. Bring to the boil, skimming off any froth that rises. Add the bay leaf, parsley and lemon juice, cover and simmer for 40 minutes.

Remove the fish heads or fish, cut off any flesh and set aside. (There's a surprising amount on fish heads – don't be put off by the look of them!)

Add the garlic, onion and tomatoes to the stock in the saucepan and simmer for 15 minutes. Transfer to a food processor or blender and process for 20 seconds. Add half the reserved fish flesh and process until smooth. Pour the mixture back into the pan and cook for 10 minutes. Season well.

Place the remaining fish flesh in individual bowls and pour over the soup. Served with good fresh bread and butter, this dish makes a generous meal in its own right.

/ CRAFTY TIP /

The Chinese have a saying that an extra guest means an extra cup of water in the soup; you can extend most soups but don't forget to add more seasoning to make up for the water.

Gratin of Onion Soup

This recipe is nearly always preceded in cookery books with tales of how the writer first had it early one morning in Les Halles, the famous fruit and vegetable market in Paris. Unfortunately, by the time I got there they were pulling Les Halles down. I have, however, managed to eat the soup in a number of French restaurants, both in France and throughout the world, and I can verify the genuine Gallic taste of this version. And you don't have to be up at 6 a.m. to taste it!

SERVES 6
25g (1 oz) beef dripping
1 kg (2 lb) onions, sliced
1 teaspoon sugar
1 dessertspoon Worcestershire sauce
1.2 litres (2 pints) beef stock
½ French loaf, cut into 1 cm (½ inch) slices
125g (4 oz) cheese (Gruyère is perfect, Gouda is fine), grated
Salt and freshly ground black pepper

Melt the dripping in a pan and fry the onions with the sugar for about 5 minutes, until they are brown but not burnt; the sugar helps to caramelise the onions and produce the rich, dark flavour and colour. Add the Worcester-shire sauce and salt and pepper to taste, pour over the stock and simmer very gently for at least 35 minutes, stirring occasionally. The onions should almost melt into the soup, but still have a slight texture of their own.

Toast the French bread lightly.

To serve, ladle the soup into heatproof dishes, float a piece of toast on top and heap the grated cheese on top of that. Place under a preheated grill for just a minute, until the cheese has melted. Serve bubbling hot, being careful not to eat it too quickly lest you singe your tongue in the excitement!

Corn Chowder

This is a vegetarian chowder, made in a similar way to the legendary fish one.

SERVES 4
2 tablespoons oil
1 onion, chopped
1 green pepper, cored, seeded and chopped
1 small can chopped tomatoes or *250 g (8 oz) fresh ones*
600ml (1 pint) chicken stock or *water*
250g (8 oz) potato, diced
500g (1 lb) sweetcorn, frozen or canned
1 tablespoon cornflour, blended with 250ml (8 fl oz) milk
Salt and freshly ground black pepper
6 cracker biscuits – cream crackers, water biscuits or Ritz crackers

Heat the oil in a pan and fry the onion and green pepper for 2 minutes. Add the tomatoes, stock or water and potato and simmer for 10 minutes. Add the sweetcorn and blended cornflour and stir over gentle heat until thickened. Season to taste and crumble the cracker biscuits over the top to serve, for the real American flavour.

Gazpacho

This soup comes from the Andalusian region of Spain. There are several versions of it, ranging from a thin, garlicky liquid with a few bits and pieces floating around, to a damp salad that couldn't be called a soup with the best will in the world! The crafty version is one of my favourites to serve on a hot summer's day, especially at a weekend buffet party. If you are a bit nervous about the garlic, you can cut down on it, but don't leave it out altogether. My recipe falls somewhere between the extremes of the do-it-yourself-dinner-party Gazpacho and the thin-as-dishwater Gazpacho, both of which have their supporters. A food processor makes this very easy.

SERVES 4–6
1 Spanish onion, finely chopped
1 clove of garlic, finely chopped
250g (8 oz) tomatoes, chopped
1 small green pepper, cored, seeded and chopped
2 tablespoons each olive oil and lemon juice

1×600ml (1 pint) can tomato juice
900ml (1½ pints) water
1 cucumber, coarsely grated with the peel left on
Salt and freshly ground black pepper
2×2.5 cm (1 inch) thick slices wholemeal bread, cut into 2.5 cm (1 inch) cubes

Place the onion, garlic, tomatoes, green pepper, oil, lemon juice and half the tomato juice in a bowl and mix well. Stir in the remaining tomato juice, water and cucumber. Season quite strongly with salt and pepper, and a pinch of sugar if the soup lacks sweetness from the tomatoes. Chill in the refrigerator for at least an hour.

To serve, ladle the soup into bowls and add a couple of ice cubes.

Place the bread cubes in a bowl for guests to serve themselves. A little grated cucumber, and chopped onion and tomato mixture in small bowls can also be served separately if you choose.

Potage Bonne Femme

The vegetable soup of France, served everywhere, was my childhood introduction to French food. A great tureen of this soup used to appear at dinner every evening in a hotel where we were staying on my first visit to a France still recovering from the ravages of war. Its rich flavour and earthy comfort have been symbolic to me ever since of the best in French cooking.

SERVES 6
250g (8 oz) each potatoes, carrots, onions and leeks
50g (2 oz) butter
1.2 litres (2 pints) chicken stock (see page 97)
Salt and freshly ground black pepper

Chop the potatoes, carrots and onion. Wash the leeks carefully and chop them finely, saving a few shreds of the green part for garnish later.

Melt the butter in a large saucepan and fry all the vegetables for about 8–9 minutes, just cooking lightly, until they and the butter absorb each other's flavours. Add salt and a good sprinkling of pepper. Pour on the stock, bring to the boil, then simmer for 20 minutes. Season to taste.

The soup is now ready to serve. You can blend it until smooth or eat it chunky. Put a knob of butter and a little finely chopped parsley into each bowl to get the perfect authentic French effect. Sprinkle the shredded green leek over the top as the soup is being served. French bread and unsalted butter complete the picture.

Creamy Spinach Soup

If pushed, this is a soup you can make without stock, and using frozen spinach. Whether you make it with fresh or frozen spinach, the butter is quite important, even though the quantity may seem generous. Spinach and butter go especially well together, and they combine to make a soup of delicate flavour and extremely beautiful colour. Even Popeye haters can fall for this.

SERVES 4

750g (1½ lb) fresh or 250g (8 oz) cooked frozen spinach
75g (3 oz) butter
300ml (½ pint) water
450ml (¾ pint) milk
1 teaspoon cornflour
Salt and freshly ground black pepper

Fresh spinach is nicest but you must wash it carefully and rough-chop it into 2.5cm (1 inch) wide ribbons, discarding any tough stalks. From there on you proceed the same way whether using fresh or frozen spinach.

Melt 50g (2 oz) of the butter in a deep saucepan, add the spinach and stir. Add the water, cover and simmer until the spinach is cooked, but not khaki – 4–5 minutes for fresh and until it's just melted for frozen spinach is right. Pour into a food processor or blender and process for 20 seconds or until the spinach is very finely chopped. You may need to stop and scrape the side of the bowl down once or twice during this process.

Return the spinach purée to the pan and add all but 2 tablespoons of the milk. Blend the cornflour to a smooth paste with the reserved milk and stir into the soup. Bring to the boil, stirring thoroughly until thickened. Season well, ladle into individual bowls and top with the reserved butter. The soup should be pale green, flecked with little specks of darker green from the spinach leaves.

CRAFTY TIP

Croûtons add a nice finishing touch to soups and add a crispness to some salads. Cut day-old bread into cubes and shallow-fry in hot oil for 1–2 minutes, until crisp and golden. Drain on absorbent paper.

Cold Apple Soup

Very unexpected to taste and easy to make, this is one of my favourite summer soups.

SERVES 4–6
500g (1 lb) cooking apples
4 tablespoons oil
1 large onion, chopped
1 tablespoon mild curry powder
900ml (1½ pints) chicken stock (see page 97)
Pinch of ground cinnamon
Salt and freshly ground black pepper

Core, but don't peel the apples, then cut into small pieces. Heat the oil in a pan, add the apple and onion and turn until coated. Add the curry powder and cook very gently for 2–3 minutes. Add the stock, bring to the boil, then simmer for 15 minutes. Pour into a food processor or blender and process until smooth. Season with a generous pinch of cinnamon and salt and pepper. Leave to cool, then place in the refrigerator until thoroughly chilled.

Serve as it is or with a generous dollop of natural yoghurt in each bowl, or with tiny cubes of unpeeled eating apple floating on the surface.

Quick Green Pea Soup

An early crafty recipe from the time when frozen peas were everywhere. Even today this is a good standby, as all the key ingredients can be kept for some months in your freezer, ready to go – there's no need to thaw them first. If you use fresh peas, simmer for an extra ten minutes.

SERVES 6–8
1.5 litres (2½ pints) chicken stock (see page 97)
500g (1 lb) frozen peas (not minted)
1 small onion, chopped
50g (2 oz) butter
1 tablespoon cornflour
Salt and freshly ground black pepper

Bring the stock to a rolling boil in a large saucepan. Add the peas and cook for 4–5 minutes. Add the onion, then the butter. When it's melted, pour into a food processor or blender and process until smooth. Return to the saucepan and season well. Blend the cornflour with a little water, add to the soup and reheat, stirring until thickened.

Add a few tablespoons of cream or top of the milk to the soup just before serving if you wish – I think it's an improvement as it helps to break down the improbably green colour that the frozen peas give. It also helps the flavour, though that's pretty good to start with.

Cock-a-leekie

This, despite its *olde worlde* funny name, is actually a very serious soup. It's part of the 'auld' alliance between Scotland and France which connected not only their royal families, but also their pattern of cooking and drinking. The use of prunes is something that's still very popular in south-western France, and though it may seem totally outrageous, works wonderfully well here, particularly if you can get a well flavoured boiling fowl as the basis of the dish.

This is customarily served in Scotland as a consommé or broth first, with the chicken, vegetables and prunes eaten afterwards, as a main course.

SERVES 4

1 × 1.1–1.3kg (2½–3 lb) roasting or, ideally, boiling chicken, cleaned
2 carrots
1kg (2 lb) leeks, split and cleaned thoroughly
1 bay leaf
250g (8 oz) prunes, soaked for at least 30 minutes in cold tea or orange
   juice
1 tablespoon chopped parsley
1 teaspoon salt
½ teaspoon freshly ground black pepper

Place the chicken, carrots, half the leeks and bay leaf in a large flameproof casserole, cover with water and simmer until the chicken is just tender. (This will take 40 minutes for a roasting chicken and at least 1½ hours for a boiling chicken.) Discard the leeks, slice the carrots and set aside.

Add the prunes and remaining leeks, finely sliced, to the broth and simmer for 20 minutes. Strain and add the parsley. Check the seasoning. Serve with the reserved sliced carrots.

As the main course, cut the chicken into joints and garnish with the prunes. Serve with the leeks in a little of the broth as the sauce. Boiled potatoes go wonderfully with this.

The London Particular

This is an adaptation of a famous nineteenth-century London soup. It is, in fact, the pea soup that the fog, also 'famous' in London at that time, was named after. The soup was traditionally made from yellow split peas, and although they are obtainable if you want to be a purist, they take a very long time to soak and cook. Not so the small red 'Egyptian' lentils, which produce a remarkably similar result. It's a soup that has the same effect as a thick overcoat in the winter – warming, comforting and very reassuring.

SERVES 6

1 tablespoon beef dripping or cooking oil
250g (8 oz) red lentils
1 large onion, sliced
Pinch of salt
1.2 litres (2 pints) beef stock
1 tablespoon molasses
1 teaspoon Worcestershire sauce
4 tablespoons croûtons

Melt the dripping or heat the oil in a heavy-based saucepan. Stir in the lentils. Add the onion and salt and stir-cook for 3–4 minutes. Add the stock, molasses and Worcestershire sauce, cover and simmer for 40 minutes, stirring occasionally. Check the seasoning and sprinkle with the croûtons to serve.

If you are alarmed by the molasses, use a smaller amount and see how you like it, but it does add a wonderful smokey, dark flavour to the soup.

Lettuce Soup

This may seem an unexpected vegetable to use for soup but, in fact, there is a long tradition of cooking lettuces that we've forgotten in this country. This soup is very light and delicate and has the extra advantage of using those bits of lettuce we normally throw away. You can make it with fresh or frozen peas (make sure frozen ones are unflavoured).

SERVES 4

50g (2 oz) butter
About 12 outer leaves of a large lettuce, cut into strips
1 bunch of spring onions
150g (5 oz) peas, fresh or frozen
600ml (1 pint) chicken stock (see page 97)
Salt and freshly ground black pepper
1 tablespoon soured cream or fromage frais

Melt the butter in a saucepan, add the lettuce, spring onions and *fresh* peas, and cook gently for 5 minutes – do not fry or allow them to brown. Season to taste, add the stock and *frozen* peas, if using, and simmer for 10 minutes. Pour into a food processor or blender and process until really smooth – there should be no lumps or bits left in this soup to have it at its full quality. Check the seasoning.

Serve hot or cold, with a swirl of soured cream or fromage frais on the top. You can also garnish it, if you like, with one of the inner leaves of the lettuce, cut into very, very thin ribbons.

Starters

Starters are the most fashionable of all courses. There's a restaurant much patronised by the Princess of Wales before her marriage that serves nothing but starters, though at main course prices. And there are some people, of whom I may be one, who think the whole of *nouvelle cuisine* is a large-scale example of the same phenomenon. That being said, I still believe that in their proper place (at the beginning of a meal) starters are not only the best way of bringing variety to your cooking, they also give you a chance to experiment without too much risk to reputation or cash.

This collection is pretty eclectic. (I'm not sure what that means, but my wife thinks it means cooking without gas.) I hope that it means a wide ranging group of recipes, from the cheap-and-cheerful right through to the posh dinner party/impress your mother-in-law/I can't afford to buy these ingredients twice to practise kind. But the key is their craftiness.

Having been rude about *nouvelle cuisine* at the start, perhaps I ought to say that some of these dishes make lovely light lunches, on their own or with a salad. And some of them go together well to make a simple version of the great Middle Eastern *mezze* – their hospitable tradition of 'eating your way through life'. It consists of a convivial meal made up of lots of tasty little dishes eaten together, cold first, then hot. If you haven't tried this style of entertaining, prepare the Leeks Provençale, Stuffed Tomatoes, Minted Cucumber Salad, Guacamole and a Chicken Liver Pâté. Add hot fresh pitta bread, a plate of fresh black olives and one of radishes, six friends and sit back and enjoy the compliments.

Kippers Michelin

I had these kippers at the launch of the first British version of the renowned *Michelin Guide* to hotels and restaurants. It just shows what an unorthodox approach can do to a food we thought we knew all about. Don't be tempted to cook the kippers – at least, not for this dish! Many shops are now selling undyed kippers, which are ideal.

SERVES 4

4 kipper fillets, sliced diagonally into 5mm (¼ inch) strips
1 Spanish onion, sliced into very thin rings
6 tablespoons oil (preferably olive)
3 tablespoons lemon juice
1 small lettuce, shredded
Freshly ground black pepper

Mix the kipper and onion together in a bowl. Cover with the oil and lemon juice and leave to marinate for at least 2 hours.

Drain and serve on a bed of lettuce, seasoned with plenty of pepper. Brown bread is best with this.

CRAFTY TIP

To fillet kippers, take the meat off the bones from the
skin side – it's easier.

Scandinavian Soused Herrings

A touch of sweet and sour makes this an unusual first course; or do as the Scandinavians do, and serve them with lots of other delicacies as part of a *smörgåsbord* spread. Herring fillets are sold in supermarkets, or ask your fishmonger to fillet the fish for you.

SERVES 4

150ml (¼ pint) cider vinegar
150 ml (¼ pint) water
2 tablespoons sugar
1 tablespoon salt
1 tablespoon pickling spice
1 onion, sliced (optional)
500g (1 lb) herring fillets
Chopped fresh herbs to garnish

Bring the vinegar and water to the boil, add the sugar and seasonings and simmer for 5 minutes. Add the onion if you wish. Cool and pour over the herrings in a flat dish and chill for 24 hours, or up to 3 days.

To serve, skin the fillets, place in a serving dish and pour over a little of the strained vinegar. Garnish with herbs – dill if you have it – and serve with rye or pumpernickel bread.

Stuffed Tomatoes

Make this simple dish in the summer and autumn when continental-style 'beef' or Marmande tomatoes are plentiful and cheap. It's quite surprising how delicious and fresh-tasting the tomatoes are, even when cooked.

SERVES 4

4 large tomatoes
50g (2 oz) fresh white breadcrumbs
1 clove of garlic, crushed with 1 teaspoon salt
1–2 spring onions, chopped
15g (½ oz) butter
50g (2 oz) chicken livers, chopped
2 tablespoons chopped parsley

Cut the tomatoes in half horizontally and scoop out the pulp. Mix together the breadcrumbs, garlic salt and spring onions.

Melt the butter in a pan and fry the livers for 1 minute. Add the breadcrumb mixture and fry for 2 minutes. Add the tomato pulp and fry for 2 minutes. Fill the tomato shells with this mixture and bake in a preheated oven, 200°C (400°F) gas mark 6, for 15 minutes. Sprinkle with the parsley and serve hot.

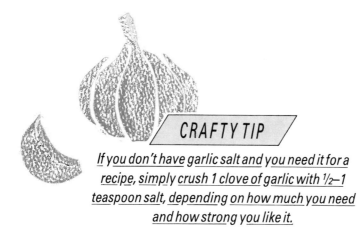

CRAFTY TIP

If you don't have garlic salt and you need it for a recipe, simply crush 1 clove of garlic with ½–1 teaspoon salt, depending on how much you need and how strong you like it.

Leeks Provençale

Leeks and lemon seem a most unlikely combination of flavours, but in fact work remarkably well. For this idea, I am indebted to Elizabeth David, as all of us who enjoy cooking in this country so often are. It's a dish that's delicious hot or cold, though I think I prefer it cold. It will keep in the refrigerator for two to three days if you cover it – a great advantage.

SERVES 4
750g (1½ lb) leeks
3 tablespoons vegetable oil
250g (8oz) can tomatoes
Grated rind and juice of 1 lemon
1 teaspoon each sugar, dried basil, dried oregano and salt

Trim the leeks, cutting off the straggly green bits, and slice into 10cm (4 inch) lengths; you should get two per leek. Clean the white part of the leeks very carefully while leaving them as whole as possible – soaking in a bowl of cold water is the best way.

Heat the oil in a pan and fry the leeks like sausages, rolling them round, for 3 minutes. Add the tomatoes and half their juice, the lemon juice and sugar, cover and simmer gently for 15–20 minutes. Add the herbs, salt and lemon rind, increase the heat and cook for 1 minute.

Serve hot for lunch with French bread and butter, or cold as a starter.

Carrots with Meaux Mustard

Carrots in France are usually associated with Vichy, down towards the south-west, but this recipe is associated with a town a bit further north called Meaux, where that lovely crunchy mustard with lots of bits in it is made. You can use bought mayonnaise or make your own (see page 27).

SERVES 4
125ml (4 fl oz) mayonnaise
1½ tablespoons Meaux whole grain mustard
500g (1 lb) carrots, grated
Small bunch of parsley, chopped

Mix the mayonnaise and mustard together, add the carrot and toss well, until thoroughly coated. Transfer to a serving dish and sprinkle with the parsley.

Don't keep this very long before eating it, although it will do perfectly well in the refrigerator for up to 6 hours.

Country Mushrooms

I first had this in Luxembourg one summer, with mushrooms I picked myself. It is an old country recipe that's very simple, quite delicious and can be made only with big mushrooms. Wild 'horse' or 'field' mushrooms are the best but, if you can find cultivated ones over 10cm (4 inches) across, they will do very well. It's a rich dish, ideal for a 'rustic' starter or for high-tea.

SERVES 4
4 large open mushrooms
125ml (4 fl oz) double cream, the thickest you can find
4 tablespoons butter
4 teaspoons chopped parsley
Salt and freshly ground black pepper

Pull the stalks from the mushrooms and wipe and trim the caps. Butter a dish large enough to hold all the mushrooms flat and arrange, black side up. Spoon 2 tablespoons of the cream onto each mushroom, top with a tablespoon of the butter and season well. Bake in a preheated oven, 220°C (425°F) gas mark 7, for 15 minutes.

Sprinkle with the parsley and pour over the pan juices. Serve with wholemeal bread.

/ **CRAFTY TIP** /

Combine a number of these salad dishes together as a party first course with radishes and good French bread. They call it crudités across the channel, but it's quite refined really.

Minted Cucumber Salad

Sliced cucumber should need no introduction in this country, where it is immortalised in tiny, brown bread and butter sandwiches with their crusts removed. In the Middle East, however, they have raised sliced cucumber to an art form.

SERVES 4
1 cucumber
1 teaspoon salt
1 sprig of mint
4 tablespoons natural yoghurt
1 teaspoon lemon juice

Hold the cucumber carefully in one hand and, taking a fork with sharp, firm prongs, run them down the length of the cucumber. Turn the cucumber round until it is all thoroughly scored. This serves two purposes: it helps the cucumber drain itself of excess liquid and provides an extremely pretty pattern when it's sliced as thinly as possible.

Sprinkle the slices with the salt and leave to drain in a colander for 30 minutes. Transfer to a serving dish, burying the mint in the middle. Just before serving, stir in the yoghurt and lemon juice.

You can serve the cucumber without draining, but it very rapidly becomes watery, even if just sitting on the table for 5 minutes.

Guacamole

This spicy avocado purée was developed in Mexico, where the avocado was first grown. It must be one of the prettiest starters, as well as pleasing most tastes. Tortilla chips, now widely available in Britain, are the traditional accompaniment, using the chips to spoon up the dip.

SERVES 4
1 tablespoon vegetable oil
2 tablespoons lemon juice
¼ teaspoon chili powder
Salt and freshly ground black pepper
2 ripe avocados
4 spring onions, finely chopped
1 each red and green pepper, cored, seeded and finely chopped
4 tomatoes, skinned and finely chopped

Mix the oil, lemon juice and seasonings together. Halve, stone and scrape out the avocados and either mash by hand or purée in a food processor or blender until smooth. Add the vegetables and oil mixture and stir well. Transfer to a serving dish.

If you have to keep it, put the stones on top and cover with clingfilm. The stones contain something that stops avocados going brown immediately they are exposed to the air.

Crab Tart

This a grand starter, both in appearance and taste. It's not cheap but can make up for a lot of other shortcuts when you're rushed, and it will set a party off to a good start. For some reason people always love tarts: don't, whatever you do, call it a quiche!

SERVES 4–6
1 quantity Shortcrust Pastry (see page 200)
2 eggs plus 1 egg yolk
250g (8 oz) crab meat (fresh or frozen)
150ml (¼ pint) single cream
Salt and freshly ground black pepper

Roll out the pastry and use to line a 20cm (8 inch) flan dish, preferably with a removable base. Prick the pastry, line the base with foil and cover with rice or beans to weigh it down. Bake in a preheated oven, 200°C (400°F) gas mark 6, for 15 minutes. Remove the foil and rice or beans. Lower the oven temperature to 190°C (375°F) gas mark 5.

Beat together the other ingredients, pour into the pastry case and return to the oven for 25 minutes.

It's marvellous served hot and all right cold, so eat it hot – there won't be many leftovers!

Smoked Salmon Quiche

A luxury dish but, happily, one which can be made with the smoked salmon off-cuts that a lot of shops sell quite cheaply. So it has an air of crafty luxury about it. Of course, if you've won the pools or live next to Harrods, you can use a whole delicately-cut slice to top the pie.

SERVES 4–6

75g (3 oz) smoked salmon pieces
150ml (¼ pint) milk
2 eggs plus 1 yolk
150ml (¼ pint) double cream
1 quantity Pâte Brisée (see page 198)
4 tablespoons grated Parmesan cheese
Salt and freshly ground black pepper

Place the smoked salmon pieces, carefully cleaned of any bone or skin, in a food processor or blender, saving one or two attractive pieces, if there are any, to decorate the top. Add the milk, eggs, egg yolk and cream. Process for about 10 seconds, until really smooth. Make sure any bits of smoked salmon left are really very fine indeed.

Line a 20cm (8 inch) flan dish with the pastry, weigh it down with foil covered with dried beans or rice, and bake in a preheated oven, 200°C (400°F) gas mark 6, for 5 minutes. Remove the foil and beans or rice and bake for another 5 minutes. Pour the smoked salmon mixture into the pastry case. Decorate with any remaining pieces of salmon. Sprinkle over the Parmesan, salt and pepper and bake for a further 10 minutes, until risen and lightly brown on the top. It is nice hot or cold.

Salad with Shrimps

If you thought shrimp cocktail was passé, reserve your judgement until you try this version with one of my favourite dressings. Even without the shrimps it's pretty good – with them a totally new experience.

SERVES 4–6

1 crisp lettuce (Webb's Wonder or Iceberg are best)
1 bunch of radishes, sliced
1 bunch of spring onions, chopped
125g (4 oz) shrimps, cooked and peeled

FOR THE DRESSING:
225ml (7 fl oz) salad oil
125ml (4 fl oz) lemon juice
50g (2 oz) blue cheese
1 teaspoon sugar
¹/₂ teaspoon salt

Break the lettuce into chunks, wash and dry it. Place in a bowl with the radishes and spring onions and arrange the shrimps on top.

Blend the dressing ingredients together in a food processor or blender, or with a rotary whisk, until smooth and creamy. Pour over the salad to serve.

Tagliatelle with Tuna Sauce

This and the following noodle dish feature the crafty 10-minute way to perfect pasta – if it seems unlikely, try it and test me. This recipe has a dead simple sauce that looks as pretty as it tastes. Green noodles are best – yellow ones are fine – white are *just* all right.

SERVES 4
250g (8 oz) tagliatelle (flat egg noodles)
300ml (¹/₂ pint) white sauce (see page 23)
1 each red and green pepper, cored, seeded and chopped
4 tablespoons chicken stock (see page 97)
25g (1 oz) butter
200g (7 oz) can tuna, drained and flaked
2 teaspoons lemon juice
2 tablespoons grated Parmesan cheese
Salt and freshly ground black pepper

Cook the noodles in plenty of boiling salted water for 3 minutes. Take off the heat, cover and leave for 7 minutes.

Meanwhile, mix the hot white sauce with the peppers, stock and seasoning to taste, then add the butter, tuna and lemon juice.

Drain the noodles, place in a serving dish, pour over the sauce and sprinkle with the Parmesan. I used to say Cheddar would do, but it really won't – you need the bite of a 'grand' cheese.

Noodles à la Crème

A very good friend of mine (famous in the broadcasting world) developed (or nicked) this recipe from a classic north Italian speciality. He always serves it at his dinner parties, calling it 'Springtime, Summer, Autumn or Winter in Tuscany', depending on the season. I suggest you do the same, but don't tell them where you got the idea – he never does! It's very easy and quite scrumptious.

SERVES 4
350g (12 oz) ribbon noodles or tagliatelle
1 egg
150ml (¼ pint) double cream
4 tablespoons grated Parmesan cheese
Salt and freshly ground black pepper

Cook the noodles in plenty of boiling salted water for 3 minutes. Take off the heat, cover and leave for 7 minutes, then drain promptly.

Beat the egg and cream together, mix with the noodles in a warm bowl and season to taste. Sprinkle with the Parmesan and eat quickly, while still hot.

Cubes of salami and/or freshly cooked green peas are sometimes added. A few flaked almonds, though not traditional, are also delicious.

CRAFTY TIP

To cook perfect pasta, boil in plenty of salted water for 3 minutes. Put on the lid, take off the heat and leave for 7 minutes, then drain promptly.

Pâtés and Pots

Pâtés present the best example of how the world has changed in the fifteen years of crafty cooking. Once upon a time, apart from the professionals, only a few brave and dedicated souls ever tried to make pâté at home. Those who did used to spend hours cutting up, mincing and blending by hand. The advent of the food processor has changed all that. What used to take one and a half hours now takes five minutes and, amazingly, the result is probably better, because none of the meat juices is lost.

There's a range of pâtés here, from the super simple to the grand, including the original crafty pâté recipe, which used liver sausage for speed! There are also some recipes for potted meats and cheese, the traditional British equivalent of pâtés, developed over many centuries. They differ from the French ones in that they happily make use of leftovers or surplus food. They are very rich and less is needed for each serving than pâtés. As modern starters or picnic food, or even sandwich fillers, they take a lot of beating.

All the recipes are made using a food processor or blender. You can make most by hand with a *mouli-légume*, mincer or pestle and mortar, but no crafty cook would try unless they *had* to.

<u>The Original Crafty Pâté</u>

Here's the original crafty pâté recipe, developed before the advent of food processors and blenders. Made with really good class calves' liver sausage and a certain insouciance, this can still be a dinner party saver if you don't have anything more 'authentic'.

SERVES 4
175g (6 oz) good calves' liver sausage
Large pinch of mixed herbs
1 teaspoon garlic salt
1 tablespoon lemon juice
75g (3 oz) butter, melted

Mash the liver sausage with the herbs, garlic salt and lemon juice. Add all but about 2 tablespoons of the butter and mix until creamy. Pack into a soufflé dish or pretty pot, smooth the top and pour over the remaining butter to seal. Chill for at least 3 hours.

Serve on hot toast or French bread baked in the oven for 10 minutes – no one will ever know!

Delicate Chicken Liver Pâté

This pâté is perfect for an occasion when a light starter is called for.

SERVES 4

75g (3 oz) butter
250g (8 oz) chicken livers (thawed if frozen)
2 eggs, beaten
3 tablespoons apple juice
Salt and freshly ground black pepper

Melt 50g (2 oz) of the butter in a thick-sided pan and turn the livers in the melted foaming butter for about 2 minutes, until brown on the outside but not hard. Place in a food processor or blender.

Melt all but 15g (½ oz) of the remaining butter in the pan and scramble the eggs until firm. Add them and the apple juice to the food processor or blender, season generously and process for 10 seconds. Scrape down the side of the bowl and process for another 10 seconds, until thoroughly mixed and very fine. Pour into a white flute-sided soufflé dish.

Melt the remaining butter, then pour it over the pâté to seal. Chill for at least 2 hours.

This is particularly nice with hot buttered toast, for it has a lovely soft, delicate spreading consistency.

CRAFTY TIP

Pâtés keep better if topped with clarified butter.
Simply melt the butter, then cook gently for about 30
seconds, without letting it turn brown. Remove
surface scum, then strain through a muslin-lined
sieve into a bowl, leaving behind any settled
sediment.

Rustic Chicken Liver Pâté

A pâté to be eaten among friends with a taste for strong, country-type foods. This is borrowed from a famous French three-star restaurant. If you can't get chicken hearts (most butchers will supply them) use all livers.

SERVES 4

125g (4 oz) chicken hearts
125g (4 oz) butter
75g (3 oz) chicken livers
2 cloves of garlic
Juice and grated rind of 1 orange
1 teaspoon each dried thyme and tarragon
Salt and freshly ground black pepper

Place the chicken hearts in a small saucepan, fill generously with water, cover and cook for 30 minutes. Drain, trim off any gristly bits and cut each heart in half. Place in a food processor or blender.

Melt all but 15g (½ oz) of the butter in the pan until foaming. Add the chicken livers and garlic and cook until the livers are browned but still slightly pink in the middle (test one to check). Add to the food processor or blender. Rinse out the pan with the orange juice and add to the food processor or blender with the orange rind, herbs and seasoning to taste. Process for 20 seconds. The mixture should still have a little texture – be a bit grainy from the tiny bits of heart in the mixture.

Pack into an oval, earthenware dish. Melt the remaining butter and pour over the top to seal. Chill overnight if you can, for the flavours to blend.

You can slice this pâté, or scoop it out of the bowl with a spoon. The centre should still be a little pink, and the flavour of the garlic and herbs should have blended thoroughly into the chicken livers.

Country Pâté

This is the most basic and simplest of all French-style pâtés – the kind usually called *Pâté du Chef* in restaurants. It is chiefly a liver pâté, flavoured with herbs and designed to be spread in large chunks on crusty bread. If you're putting a picnic together, take some with you, still in its terrine, and use a spoon to serve it onto the bread. A good grainy French mustard goes extremely well, or dill-flavoured gherkins make a nice sharp contrast to its richness.

SERVES 6–8

2 × 2.5 cm (1 inch) thick slices of bread, crumbed
1 large onion, quartered
500g (1 lb) calves' or lambs' liver, cut into 2.5cm (1 inch) cubes
125g (4 oz) beef kidney fat or suet, cut into 2.5cm (1 inch) cubes
1 teaspoon each chopped thyme and oregano
2 eggs
2 bay leaves
Salt and freshly ground black pepper

Place the breadcrumbs and onion in a food processor or blender and process for about 10 seconds, to purée. Transfer to a bowl.

Process the liver and beef fat or suet for 20 seconds. Scrape down the side of the bowl and add the herbs and a generous amount of salt and pepper. With the motor running, add the eggs, one at a time. Add the bread and onion mixture and process until thoroughly mixed.

Pack into an oval terrine which will fit inside a baking dish and place the bay leaves on top. Fill the baking dish with water 2.5cm (1 inch) deep, place the terrine in it and cook in a preheated oven, 180°C (350°F) gas mark 4, for 1 hour, until the sides have shrunk away from the terrine a little. If you like, cover the pâté with a sheet of foil placed lightly over the top.

Leave it to cool for at least 12 hours, weighed down with a plate and a couple of large cans from the larder. When cool, cover with clingfilm and it will keep in the refrigerator for over a week, or for 4 days once it's been cut.

Smoked Mackerel Pâté

Smoked mackerel are one of the crafty gourmet delicacies – still about the cheapest fish we have, yet tasting as fine, or finer to my mind, than most smoked salmon. When you are making this pâté, which has become a firm favourite in restaurants, choose mackerel that are not too brightly coloured – they should have been turned a golden brown by smoke and not bright yellow by chemical dyes. There are even some fishmongers these days who are smoking their own. Also on the market are Scandinavian-style home smokers, about the size of a shoe box, that produce quite delicious smoked fish at the expense of some time and effort – both may be worth it.

SERVES 6
250g (8 oz) smoked mackerel (fillets are fine)
125g (4 oz) cream cheese (either fresh or fromage frais)
1 lemon
¼ teaspoon nutmeg
½ teaspoon freshly ground black pepper
50g (2 oz) butter, melted
Salt

Skin and carefully bone the mackerel, place in a food processor or blender with the cream cheese, the juice of half the lemon, and seasonings. Process for 10 seconds, scrape down the side of the bowl and process again until the mixture is thoroughly smooth and blended. (If you wish, add 1 slice of bread soaked in milk at this stage for a lighter flavour and texture.) With the motor running, add half the butter. Pack into individual ramekins or a large soufflé dish.

Slice the remaining lemon very thinly, removing any pips, and lay in an overlapping pattern around the top of the pâté, or place one slightly thicker slice on each ramekin. Pour the remaining butter over the top to seal and chill for at least 2 hours before serving.

Salmon Pâté

Incredibly rich, yet amazingly crafty – this is one of the grandest dishes I know. A special start for that special meal. It was taught to me by an actress who brought the 'X' appeal to *Z-Cars*. A food processor or blender makes this too smooth for my taste, but do use one if you wish.

SERVES 6
500g (1 lb) salmon
250g (8 oz) unsalted butter, melted
2 tablespoons lemon juice
4 tablespoons chopped parsley
Salt and freshly ground black pepper

Place the salmon in a saucepan, just cover with boiling water, cover and cook for 5 minutes. Leave to cook in the liquid for 2 hours, then skin, bone and flake into a bowl. Stir in all but about 2 tablespoons of the butter, add the lemon juice, parsley and season to taste. Stir well to mix, transfer to a soufflé dish and pour the remaining butter over the top to seal. Chill for at least 2 hours before serving with lots of hot brown toast.

Smoked Haddock Mousse

An early 'crafty' mousse that's always a favourite, even with 'difficult' guests. Serve with a big spoon straight from the dish, with a lemon quarter for each guest to squeeze over their helping.

SERVES 4
500g (1 lb) smoked haddock
150ml (¼ pint) milk
150ml (¼ pint) water
1 tablespoon flour
25g (1 oz) butter
4 tablespoons mayonnaise
1 tablespoon lemon juice
Salt and freshly ground black pepper

Place the haddock, milk and water in a saucepan, cover and cook for 8 minutes, until tender. Remove the fish from the pan, reserving the liquid. Skin and bone the fish and flake finely with a fork into a bowl. Whisk the flour and butter into the cooking liquid and bring to the boil, when it will thicken. Add to the fish, season to taste (go easy on the salt) and stir in the mayonnaise and lemon juice. Transfer to a soufflé dish, smooth the top and chill for at least 2 hours. Granary toast is fabulous with this.

CRAFTY TIP

If you haven't got any French or crusty bread use an eighteenth-century trick called 'pulled bread'. Just tear half a loaf into cup-sized pieces and put them into a hot oven for 10 minutes. They come out transformed and crispy.

Courgette Pâté

A real dish of the '1980s' – vegetarian, light and yet surprisingly luscious. The recipe comes, slightly 'craftified', from a friend called Glenda, whom I hope will excuse the liberty.

SERVES 4
125g (4 oz) butter
½ an onion, chopped
350g (12 oz) courgettes, cut into 1 cm (½ inch) slices
2 eggs, beaten
1 tablespoon chopped parsley
Salt and freshly ground black pepper

Melt half the butter in a frying pan and sauté the onion for 2 minutes, until just soft. Add the courgettes, turn in the butter and simmer for 3 minutes. Purée in a food processor or blender.

Melt the remaining butter in the pan and scramble the eggs until firm. Add to the courgette purée with the parsley and process again. Season generously, pot and chill the pâté for at least 2 hours – it will be firm, but not sliceable. Serve with crusty wholemeal bread.

Potted Turkey

Perfect for post-Christmas use of the inevitable turkey bits, especially as the scraps you otherwise can't find a use for go perfectly into this dish. As most people will have had their fill of turkey by the time you get round to making this, why not freeze it? A couple of months later it may prove a revelation which excites praise and smiles instead of groans and head-holding the day after Boxing Day.

SERVES 4–6

1 slice of white bread or 2 tablespoons stuffing
250g (8 oz) turkey scraps (some skin will do, though it shouldn't
 be all skin)
2–3 tablespoons giblet stock, gravy or water
½ teaspoon each salt and freshly ground black pepper
2 tablespoons cranberry sauce (if available)
125g (4 oz) butter, melted

Put the bread or stuffing into a food processor or blender and process for 2 or 3 seconds until crumbed. Add the other ingredients, except the butter, and process for about 15 seconds, until a fine purée forms. Scrape down the side of the bowl once or twice. With the motor running, add the butter through the feed tube, until thoroughly blended. Transfer to individual bowls or one large soufflé dish and chill until required.

If serving fairly soon, a teaspoon of cranberry sauce piled in the middle with a couple of holly sprigs makes an attractive decoration. Don't freeze it with the holly on though – it won't taste nice and it'll make holes in the clingfilm!

Potted Tongue

If you ever cook tongues yourself and slice them, hot or cold, you may find yourself with bits left over. These are perfect for this recipe, as are scraps left from shop-bought tongues, or even a quarter bought specially for the purpose. There's a very meaty flavour to this recipe, and it goes especially well with old-fashioned English-type chutneys, or mustard a little stronger than the French care for. Do not add any salt – the tongue, and possibly even the butter, have more than enough salt in them already.

SERVES 4
175g (6 oz) cooked tongue (cut up if in large chunks)
½ teaspoon each freshly ground black pepper and mustard powder
1 dessertspoon redcurrant jelly
Generous pinch of ground allspice
125g (4 oz) unsalted or mildly salted butter, melted

Place all the ingredients, except the butter, in a food processor or blender and process for about 10 seconds. With the motor running, pour the butter through the feed tube and blend thoroughly.

Scrape out the bowl carefully and pack the potted meat into individual ramekins or small dishes. Chill for about 2 hours, until set. It will keep, covered, for nearly a week in the refrigerator. Serve with brown toast.

Potted Cheese

The very ordinariness of the ingredients makes even more surprising the piquancy and creamy texture of this special spread. It can be used to turn 'heels' of stale-ish cheese into a simple starter.

SERVES 2
125g (4 oz) Cheddar or Double Gloucester cheese, grated
50g (2 oz) butter, melted
1 tablespoon lemon juice
½ tablespoon ground mace
½ tablespoon prepared English mustard

Mash all the ingredients together thoroughly and pack into a small soufflé dish. Melt a little extra butter to pour over the top to seal. Chill for about 2 hours, until set. Serve with brown toast.

A little mango chutney in it isn't authentic – but very tangy! Try about 2 teaspoons.

Eggstraordinary

The really extraordinary thing about eggs is how versatile and adaptable they are and how much we under-rate them. Whole meals or light snacks, grand concoctions or simple sarnies – eggs make them all easy and 'eggsciting'. In many ways we take eggs too much for granted; egg and chips is almost a synonym for not trying in the kitchen, while soft-boiled eggs – at their best a great delicacy – we think of as nursery fare. This is strange because not only do we use eggs all the time in so many dishes, but they can in some recipes be one of the most severe tests of cooking skill. I know one famous chef whose only test for an applicant assistant is to make an omelette.

In broadcasting terms, eggs have been the scene of both my triumphs and unquestionably my greatest disasters! One or two of the more successful ideas are represented below: the Smoked Salmon Scramble is terrific for tea and Caroline's Cheese Pudding is a reputation-saver from the fridge when something has gone wrong with plan 'A'.

But back to the disasters, just in case you thought I was dodging. The first was on my very first television appearance. It was on HTV's afternoon programme *Women Only*. I was cooking a Spanish omelette and had practised for days at home getting every move right. Unfortunately, when it came to the performance I discovered that I had left one crucial thing out of my calculations . . . I would be cooking on electricity not gas! All my timing was shot to pieces and I had a choice of burned or raw Spanish omelette. I chose raw – you can always say it will cook later.

The other mega-shambles was years later on TV AM. By this time I had done quite a lot of telly, but little of it live at seven in the morning. I hadn't learned to give myself the five minute safety margin that live television demands. When cooking a Yorkshire pudding due to be ready on screen at 9.05, I planned it to be *ready* at 9.05. So when Angela Rippon strolled over at 5 minutes *to* 9 and began the item, neither the pudding nor I were ready. I will never forget the sight of the flattest pancake south of Bradford and Angela's only too accurate observation on cutting it: 'Ooooooh it's oooozing'!

I hope that no such catastrophe will befall you in this collection of ideas that ranges from the reborn Spanish omelette into more 'eggsistential' realms.

The Ultimate Omelette

I ate the ultimate omelette when just eighteen years old, travelling by train to Spain. The chef served me, and a restaurant car full of other people, with this dish for breakfast. It was an omelette crisp and golden on the outside and soft and melting at the centre.

I've spent nearly twenty years of my life since trying to discover the secret. I've tried free-range eggs, whipping not beating the mixture, salted and unsalted butter, everything – and had little success though plenty of omelettes! I discovered quite recently that it's not what you put in the omelette that matters, so much as what you put the omelette *in*. The big shallow pans sold as omelette pans that I was using were the problem. For 3 eggs the secret is never to use a pan bigger than 13cm (5 inches). If that seems tiny, it is but it works. For 6 eggs use an 18cm (7 inch) pan, 10 eggs in a 25cm (10 inch) pan, and at least a dozen for a 30cm (12 inch). It's the *depth* of egg mixture, you see, that makes the difference. Follow the recipe instructions and if you can't hear the click of the wheels on the Chemin de Fer en route for Barcelona, it's not my fault.

Any filling – creamed spinach, sautéed mushrooms, cubes of cheese or croûtons – must be prepared in advance and added to the omelette just before folding and serving. The whole process shouldn't take more than 2 minutes – if it does, something's wrong.

If you want a bigger omelette increase the volume of both pan and eggs, but don't increase the time very much.

SERVES 1

3 eggs
1 tablespoon butter
Salt and freshly ground black pepper

Beat the eggs until they're well mixed. (Add *no* milk or cream.) Heat a 13cm (5 inch) pan until it's *hot*. Add the butter and swirl round until it stops sizzling. Pour in the eggs and scramble with a fork over high heat until they start to set all through. Cook for about 45 seconds, until the base is solid, then season generously. Add 2 teaspoons *only* of your chosen filling, then fold in half. Tip the pan and roll the omelette out onto a warm plate. Serve immediately.

Spanish Omelette

Spanish omelettes are a family favourite and an absolutely essential part of Saturday lunchtime, partly because of a crafty desire to use up leftovers. It is possible, however, to use special ingredients, which turn it into a really tasty and visually attractive dish. It's best served straight from the frying pan, cut into large wedges, rather like a cake. Served with crusty wholemeal bread and cheese and fruit to follow it makes a good meal for the hungriest of families.

SERVES 4

500g (1 lb) potatoes, boiled and sliced
1 onion, chopped
50g (2 oz) salami or similar meat, coarsely chopped, or tuna, flaked
2 tablespoons oil
125g (4 oz) mixed vegetables, canned, frozen or leftovers
25g (1 oz) butter
8 eggs, beaten
1 tomato, thinly sliced
Salt and freshly ground black pepper

Mix together the potato, onion and meat or tuna. Heat the oil in a 25–30cm (10–12 inch) frying pan and fry the potato mixture gently for 3–4 minutes, until the onion is softened and the whole has a few flecks of crisp brown. Turn it over regularly. Add the vegetables and cook for 3 minutes.

Turn up the heat and add the butter. When melted, pour in the seasoned eggs, scrambling and mixing the whole panful together until the eggs start to set. Lower the heat and leave until it's cooked through, about 4 minutes. You can put it under the grill for 1 minute if you wish.

Arrange the tomato on the omelette to serve.

VARIATION

Sausage Omelette

This recipe stretches 250g (8 oz) sausages to feed 4 people. Fry the sausages carefully until they are cooked through and brown, but not burst and burnt. Cut in half lengthways. Proceed as above, leaving out the salami or tuna, and when the omelette is almost set, arrange the sausages like spokes in a wheel with the tomato slices between them. A favourite with the children, this one – pretty good for their parties, too.

Lemony Eggs with Shrimps

Derived from an Arab technique with eggs, this is pretty and pungent; it is good as the hot part of a mixed hors-d'œuvres.

SERVES 4
25g (1 oz) butter
1 clove of garlic, chopped
8 eggs, beaten
1 tablespoon lemon juice
125g (4 oz) peeled shrimps or prawns
Salt and freshly ground black pepper

TO SERVE:
4 slices of hot buttered toast, crusts removed
4 unpeeled shrimps or prawns

Melt the butter in a pan and add the garlic. Add the eggs and scramble until they are soft *but not set*. Stir in the lemon juice and season to taste. *Still do not let the eggs set*. Add the peeled shrimps or prawns. Pile onto the toast, garnish with the shrimps or prawns and serve hot.

Pipérade

From the Basque regions of France and Spain comes one of the nicest and simplest of starters. Don't let the eggs get too hard – it can still taste okay but the texture won't make the same creamy sauce for the crisp, bright vegetables. It can be eaten cold, too, and is nice in little tartlets as part of an hors-d'œuvres.

SERVES 4

4 tablespoons oil (olive is ideal)
1 onion, sliced
1 each red and green pepper, seeded and sliced
4 tomatoes, sliced
6 eggs
½ teaspoon paprika
Salt and freshly ground black pepper

Heat the oil in a large frying pan and fry the onion and peppers for 5 minutes. Add the tomatoes and cook for 5 minutes. Break the eggs and stir into the mixture, without beating first. Season with salt, pepper and paprika (*not* chili pepper). Stir until the eggs are creamy but not hard. Serve at once.

Eggs Florentine

Creamy eggs, rich spinach and a smooth cheesy sauce all come together from one of the most sumptuous cuisines in the whole of Italy. This is a starter to serve with a little Vivaldi in the background and your best Botticelli on the wall behind you. But even the Eurythmics and a British Airways calendar won't distract from the taste!

SERVES 4

4 eggs
25g (1 oz) butter
1kg (2 lb) fresh or 500g (1 lb) frozen spinach (thawed)
Pinch of ground nutmeg
4 tablespoons grated Parmesan cheese
Salt and freshly ground black pepper

Creamy Spinach Soup (below)
Greek Lemon Soup (bottom)

FOR THE SAUCE:
2 tablespoons flour
600ml (1 pint) milk
50g (2 oz) butter

Put the eggs in boiling water for exactly 5 minutes, then place in cold water. Shell carefully – the yolks are still soft!

Melt the butter in a large pan and fry the spinach until soft and dryish.

To make the sauce, blend the flour with a little of the milk. Place it in a saucepan with the butter and remaining milk and bring to the boil, whisking gently until it thickens. Mix half the sauce with the cooked spinach and place in a gratin or flat baking dish. Season well and sprinkle with the nutmeg.

Place the eggs on the spinach and cover with the remaining sauce and the Parmesan cheese. Place under a hot grill for 2 minutes only, until sizzling. Serve immediately. Wholemeal bread is nice for scraping the plates.

CRAFTY TIP

To poach eggs easily: add a spoonful of vinegar to the water; when it boils stir in one direction to make a mini whirlpool, and slide in an egg off a saucer. It makes all the difference.

Eggs en Cocotte

This is a classic part of French cooking that's so easy we have it for a light supper at the end of a hard day. You can find miniature frying pan-shaped ceramic dishes to cook these, but little soufflé-type bowls are okay.

SERVES 4
4 teaspoons butter
4 large eggs
4 tablespoons double cream
4 tablespoons grated Parmesan cheese

Butter each dish and break in an egg. Pour 1 tablespoon cream around each egg, then sprinkle with the cheese and remaining butter, cut into slices.

Put 1cm (½ inch) water in a frying pan with a lid. Bring to the boil, carefully place the dishes in the pan, cover and boil for 3–4 minutes. Make sure the water doesn't come over the edge of the dishes. Serve at once.

Stuffed Three Delicious

A Chinese-style name for one of the simplest and most delicious of all egg recipes. If you don't have the exact ingredients, you can always improvise, but keep the colours separate.

SERVES 6
6 hard-boiled eggs
50g (2 oz) can anchovies, drained and mashed
1 tablespoon tomato purée
2 tablespoons mango chutney
1 tablespoon grainy French mustard
1 tablespoon mayonnaise
Chopped parsley to garnish

Halve the eggs lengthways, remove the yolks and divide between 3 bowls, that is, 2 egg yolks in each bowl. Add the anchovies and tomato purée to one bowl, the chutney to the next, and the mustard and mayonnaise to the third. Blend each until smooth, then spoon back into the whites, mounding up the filling. Sprinkle with parsley.

Serve one of each flavour per person, with French bread.

CRAFTY TIP

To stop eggs bursting when you boil them, pierce the fat end with a needle or pin before putting into the hot water.

Smoked Salmon Scramble

This trick with smoked salmon is an example of how food processors make a little luxury go a long way. I serve it as a favourite starter for special parties, either on a carefully stamped out toast round (crusts removed and cut with one of those crinkly-edged cutters) or piled into delicate china bowls.

Many shops that sell smoked salmon have packages of cheap off-cuts which are fine for this, as it's the flavour not the long, thin slices that matter.

SERVES 6
125g (4 oz) smoked salmon
6 eggs
1 tablespoon lemon juice
50g (2 oz) butter
1 tablespoon chopped parsley
Salt and freshly ground black pepper

Set aside half the salmon and cut into matchstick slivers. Place the remainder in a food processor or blender with the eggs, lemon juice and seasoning to taste. Process for 5 seconds, scrape down the side of the bowl and process again until the salmon is chopped extremely finely into the egg mixture.

Melt the butter in a heavy-based saucepan (please don't be stingy with it, the quantity is important). When it's melted but not browned at all, add the egg mixture and scramble gently, stirring with a wooden spoon until soft and creamy but not set hard; it will go on cooking when you take it off the heat.

Mix in the reserved salmon and pile onto buttered toast rounds or into small china ramekins, or even giant egg cups. Sprinkle with the parsley and serve quickly, while it's still piping hot.

'That' Yorkshire Pudding

Here's that fateful Yorkshire pudding (see page 60)! Despite the humiliation on TV AM, it has never failed me before or since, so I commend it to your attention. I am indebted to Jane Grigson for the method who in turn, I believe, had it from the then *Manchester Guardian*.

SERVES 4
300ml (½ pint) milk
4 eggs
½ teaspoon salt
Pinch of pepper
250g (8 oz) plain flour, sifted

Mix the milk, eggs and seasoning together, beating well. Leave to stand for 15 minutes, then whisk in the flour.

Pour some dripping from the meat, if you're roasting beef, or some cooking oil if you're not, into a small 25 × 15cm (10 × 6 inch) roasting pan and place in a preheated oven, 230°C (450°F) gas mark 8. When it's hot, pour in the batter and cook for just over 20 minutes. The pudding will rise spectacularly and be crisp and golden.

Caroline's Cheese Pudding

Soufflés have always been a matter of much mystery to me. It's not that I can't make them, I'm just not quite sure why to bother, because they always seem to be so insubstantial that one goes chasing after them rather like clouds, never quite catching up with either their texture or taste. This dish is a primitive soufflé, taught to me by an old friend called Caroline. While there's nothing insubstantial about this dish, in its texture or flavour, the ingredients must make it one of the cheapest family favourites on record. A food processor or blender is really needed for the breadcrumbs.

SERVES 4

2 thick slices of bread (stale is okay as long as it's not rock hard),
  crumbed
125g (4 oz) cheese, grated
2 eggs, separated
300ml (½ pint) milk
Salt and freshly ground black pepper

Mix the breadcrumbs and cheese together lightly. Add the egg yolks and milk and season generously.

Whip the egg whites with a beater until stiff but not grainy, then fold carefully into the mixture. Pile into a deep buttered baking dish (the sides must be at least 2.5cm [1 inch] higher than the mixture) and cook in a preheated oven, 190°C (375°F) gas mark 5, for approximately 45 minutes, until a skewer or sharp knife, slid into the middle, comes out clean. It'll rise, though not so spectacularly as a true soufflé, the top will go brown and bubbly and there will be a delicious cheesy smell coming from the oven.

Eat it quickly, with perhaps a green salad or fruit to follow.

VARIATION

I'm particularly fond of this, although Caroline hasn't authorised it: add a handful of chopped fresh herbs – parsley, marjoram and chives are my favourites. The herbs stay green and add a lovely fresh, country flavour to the whole pudding. Dried herbs don't seem to work quite so well.

Grains, Pulses and Pasta

This is really a hotch-potch chapter because, although grains, pulses and pasta are usually grouped together in cookery books, there's no real reason for it. They come from all over the world and are used in all sorts of different ways. The thing that really unites them is that together they form a central part of any vegetarian or low meat diet.

Maize and beans, for example, which both developed in the third millennium BC in Mexico, provide, with the vegetables that normally go with them – tomatoes, red and green peppers and avocados – an extremely balanced diet without the need for any meat or additional fat. When maize crossed the Atlantic to Africa and initially the beans, tomatoes and so forth did not, a new disease appeared on the west and then the east coasts of Africa that became known as mealies (disease). It was caused by people changing from their traditional foods to the more easily grown maize. And without the other ingredients to balance their diet, they suffered from intense forms of protein deficiency diseases and scurvy. Thus – grains and pulses go together on this occasion, with a little pasta thrown in!

Rice

There are many different kinds of rice, all of which, until very recently, was always eaten polished. The passion for brown rice that's latterly developed is an extremely modern and really quite a western thing. There's very little tradition of it in any of the countries where rice forms the staple part of the diet. In fact, brown rice has remarkably little fibre in it – the husk contains only a small additional mineral and vitamin content, so perhaps the people in the Far East knew more than we, as brown rice is certainly harder to cook and takes much longer than white or polished rice. Good brown rice, though, does provide a different flavour and texture – nuttier and munchier.

The main differences between rices are in shape. These range from the extremely thin long grain Basmati rice, grown around the foothills of the Himalayas and fragrant on its own, through the slightly shorter grained Patna and American 'long grain' rices, to the Italian-style fat, medium grain Arborio, used for risottos and the very short grain rice that used to be called

Carolina rice (as it was mostly grown in that part of the United States in the eighteenth and nineteenth centuries) we use for rice puddings.

The longer the grain the more likely the rice is to stay in one piece as it cooks. The Chinese and Japanese use a medium grain rice but cook it in a different way in order to produce the clinging stickiness that makes it easier to eat with chopsticks.

I've given a method for cooking rice the way the Indians and people in the Middle East eat it, a Chinese/Japanese technique and a pilau rice – one of the wonderful, fragrant confections to be found in the great culinary triangle between Cairo, Istanbul and Dhaka. Pilaus are lovely single-dish meals of rice blended with nuts, fruit, meat, spices and saffron, that produce superb flavours known locally by names as varied as Paolo and Biriani.

Indian/Persian Rice

This is the kind of rice that, when cooked, has each grain separate and is designed to be eaten with the rich, spicy meat or vegetable stews and curries of the region.

SERVES 4
250g (8 oz) Basmati or long grain Patna-style rice
1 teaspoon each salt and oil
25g (1 oz) butter

Rinse the rice in a sieve under running cold water for about 1 minute, until the water starts to run clear. Place it in a large saucepan with 2.25 litres (4 pints) water and add the salt and oil. Leave to soak for 5 minutes, then bring to the boil. Simmer for 8–10 minutes, testing the rice at 8 minutes: it should be firm but without a hard centre to the grain. As soon as it's cooked, drain it into a sieve and pour 1.2 litres (2 pints) hot or boiling water through the rice to strain away any remaining starch. Return it to the saucepan with the butter, put the lid on, give it a shake and leave to stand for 5 minutes, to absorb the butter. It will keep warm in the saucepan for another 10–15 minutes with the lid on.

Chinese-Style Rice

This is the way to cook rice if you're going to eat it with chopsticks or with the kind of thick-sauced, thinly-sliced food that's traditionally associated with South-east Asia, China and Japan. The intention here is not to wash the starch away, but to make sure the rice has a certain amount of cling, so that the grains don't separate too easily when they're picked up.

SERVES 4

*1 × 300ml (½ pint) mug filled with medium to long grain rice (measured
    by volume)*
1 teaspoon each salt and oil

Place the rice, salt and oil in a saucepan with a close-fitting lid. Add double the volume of water (that is, 2 mugs) and bring to the boil. Turn to the lowest heat possible, cover and leave for 12 minutes, by which time the rice should have absorbed all the liquid and be dry on top with little pock-mark holes dotted all over its surface. Put a piece of absorbent paper or a clean tea towel across the top of the saucepan, re-fit the lid and leave the rice to steam for another 5 minutes on the lowest possible heat, or in a warm place.

When you serve it, the rice will come out in little clumpy balls which can be smoothed out with a fork if you want to, but are meant to hold together as part of the chopsticks revolution.

VARIATION

Brown rice can be cooked in exactly the same way. Add an extra half-cup of water and stir thoroughly just after it's come to the boil. Cook for 5–10 minutes longer and steam for an extra 5–10 minutes.

Grains

Celebratory Chicken Biriani

This is one of the festive dishes that exists in a variety of forms in the area bounded by the Bay of Bengal and eastern Mediterranean and the Himalayas. It's been eaten for centuries with very little change in each region's methods, although the names and one or two of the refinements do vary. In a biriani the rice is boiled before mixing with the other ingredients. In a pilau all the ingredients are fried first, including the rice, before adding the liquid.

This is a 'crafty' recipe, made rather more simply than some of the grand versions, which I've seen cooked in pots big enough to get a modern microwave oven in and put the lid on. If you don't have, or fancy buying, the various spices, use a tablespoon of *good* mild curry powder instead.

SERVES 4

250g (8 oz) Basmati or long grain rice
1 tablespoon oil
50g (2 oz) butter
1 large onion, sliced
2 cloves of garlic, sliced
1 × 1.3kg (3 lb) roasting chicken, cut into 8 pieces
1 teaspoon each ground coriander, turmeric and ginger
3/4 teaspoon each chili powder, cinnamon and cloves
1/2 teaspoon each ground cumin seed and salt
1 small packet powdered or whole saffron
125g (4 oz) slivered almonds
25g (1 oz) sultanas

Rinse the rice thoroughly in a sieve under running cold water. Place it in a saucepan with 2.25 litres (4 pints) water and a pinch of salt, bring to the boil and cook for just 6 minutes. Drain and set aside.

Meanwhile, heat the oil and half the butter in a pan and fry the onion and garlic until well browned. Add the chicken and stir and turn for 1 minute. Add all the spices, except the saffron, and the salt and continue to stir for 2–3 minutes over a gentle heat, until the spices give off a rich fragrance. Add enough water to cover, bring to the boil and simmer very fast until the liquid has almost all gone.

Place half the rice in a large casserole and place the chicken curry on top. Spoon the rest of the rice over, cover and cook in a preheated oven, 180°C (350°F) gas mark 4, for 40 minutes.

Dissolve the saffron in a cup of hot water and pour it evenly across the top of the rice. Put the lid back on and cook for another 10 minutes.

Melt the remaining butter in a small pan and fry the almonds and sultanas until lightly golden.

Spoon the biriani into a large serving bowl, mixing the rice and chicken curry thoroughly, and sprinkle with the almonds and sultanas. Serve with chutneys and a yoghurt and cucumber mint salad.

The smell of the spices, the softness of the chicken, the richness of the rice and the crunchiness of the almonds make a wonderful combination.

Couscous

Couscous is a form of very fine cracked wheat that looks a bit like semolina. The staple dish of north Africa, it was traditionally made in the home, but these days it's widely available in health food shops and supermarkets, bought in from experts who make it with the help of a few machines.

The sauces it's customarily eaten with vary from region to region: in Tunisia they favour fish and the bright colourings of tomato; in Morocco, lamb dishes with a subtle combination of spices; and further east, vegetarian food often rules the roost. This recipe uses the traditional number of vegetables in such a vegetarian Couscous – namely seven.

SERVES 4
500g (1 lb) couscous
2 large onions
250g (8 oz) each courgettes, carrots and green beans
1 tablespoon olive oil
1 small cauliflower, broken into florets
250g (8 oz) cooked chick peas (canned are fine)
1 clove of garlic, crushed
1/2 teaspoon each cinnamon, turmeric and salt
25g (1 oz) butter (optional)

Place the couscous in a bowl and add a cup of cold water. Stir with a fork, letting the water soak up completely. Add another cup of water and repeat the process, making sure the couscous doesn't form into lumps. Place in a fine sieve or colander which will fit into a saucepan with the lid on the top.

Slice the onions, courgettes and carrots into 5mm (1/4 inch) thick slices.

Heat the oil and fry the onions, carrots and cauliflower florets, until softened. Add the chick peas, garlic, spices and salt and enough water to cover by 2.5cm (1 inch). Bring to a gentle boil, place the sieve or colander of couscous on top and cover with a lid. Cook for about 10–15 minutes, until the vegetables are done, then add the courgettes and beans and cook for 5 minutes.

To serve, stir the butter, if using, into the couscous, then transfer to a bowl. Make a well in the middle, put the vegetables into it and add 1–2 tablespoons of the sauce. Serve the rest separately. A pinch of chili powder and a crushed small clove of garlic in the sauce jug turn the sauce into a crafty version of Harissa – the only onomatopoeic sauce I know, because that's the noise you make if you take a little too much of it at a time!

Bulgur Pilau

This is a grain that's very popular in what used to be called Asia Minor – that bit of the world north of the eastern Mediterranean and south of the Urals, which is now mostly part of the Union of Soviet Socialist Republics. Bulgur wheat is made from cracked whole wheat, broken down into grains about the size of rice. It can be used in a variety of different ways and there are the most wonderful recipes for mixing it with walnuts, stuffing pheasants and cooking them in pomegranate sauce – a little complicated, however, for real 'crafty' cooking. This simple recipe would probably be eaten in its homeland of northern Anatolia with a rich, spicy vegetable stew containing aubergines, onions, carrots and garlic, possibly courgettes and pumpkin, and certainly some chili pepper.

SERVES 4
2 tablespoons olive oil
1 clove of garlic
1 small onion, chopped very finely
350g (12 oz) bulgur wheat
2 cardamom pods
1 small piece of cinnamon stick
600ml (1 pint) water or chicken stock
25g (1 oz) butter
50g (2 oz) pine nuts
Salt and freshly ground black pepper

Heat the oil in a pan with a close-fitting lid, and cook the garlic and onion gently without browning. Add the bulgur wheat and turn until coated in the oil. Add the cardamom and cinnamon and season to taste. Pour in the water or stock – it should come approximately 2.5cm (1 inch) above the level of the bulgur wheat. Bring to the boil, turn down to the lowest possible heat (you may want to use a heat diffuser), cover and cook very gently for 15–18 minutes, until the liquid is totally absorbed. Put a piece of absorbent paper or a clean tea towel between the lid and the bulgur wheat and fit the lid on again tightly. Leave to stand for 5 minutes.

Meanwhile, melt the butter in a small pan and fry the pine nuts gently until pale gold.

Transfer the pilau to a serving bowl, stirring it with a fork to break down any lumps, sprinkle with the pine nuts and serve immediately. It is a marvellous alternative to rice with a large number of dishes.

Pulses

This is the collective name for dried beans and lentils. There are numerous types, in a variety of shapes, sizes and colours – red, white, green, even black. The Japanese have tiny ones not much bigger than the size of a pinhead called aduki, and in parts of Peru there is a kind of lima bean that comes out nearly 2.5cm (1 inch) long dried, and twice that size when it's soaked.

Soaking is the key to all bean cooking. All pulses need a good solid soaking before they can be cooked – at least 4 hours, preferably 6–12 – to allow them to absorb as much water as possible. Never salt them while soaking. The method of cooking is the same for all beans, though some need a longer cooking time. The only exceptions are red or Egyptian lentils that can be cooked immediately.

Soak 500g (1 lb) beans for at least 6 hours in plenty of cold water. Drain and place in a large saucepan. Cover with fresh cold water to at least 3.5cm (1½ inches) above the beans. Bring to the boil and boil vigorously for 10 minutes, then part cover and simmer for 40 minutes to 1½ hours, depending on the size of the beans and their age. You can tell they're tender when a bean crushes easily between finger and thumb (or fork and the side of the saucepan).

At this point you can let them cool to be used on another occasion, or use them for making soup, chili con carne or any of a wide variety of other dishes – my two favourites follow.

Beans and Cream

This dish was designed originally for those very delicate pale green beans called flageolets which come from the French town of Soissons. They're supposed to be the most delicate and flavoursome of all dried beans and their price certainly reflects this, but cooked like this I think they're worth it – and the extra care. I used to serve this dish as part of a main course, usually with roast lamb and Pommes de Terre Dauphinoise (see page 173), but people like it so much that now I tend to serve it on its own after the lamb and potatoes.

SERVES 4
250g (8 oz) dried flageolets, soaked as described on page 75 for at least 6
    hours then drained
1 teaspoon ground nutmeg
50g (2 oz) butter
4 sticks of celery, thinly sliced
125ml (4 fl oz) thick double cream
Salt and freshly ground black pepper

Put the beans, nutmeg and half the butter in a tall, preferably earthenware, casserole and cover with water to 2.5cm (1 inch) above the beans. Cover and cook in a preheated oven, 180°C (350°F) gas mark 4, until all the water has been absorbed by the beans; if they're fairly fresh (this season's beans) this should take about 1 hour, but it might take up to 1½ hours. Keep warm.

Melt the remaining butter in a frying pan and quickly stir fry the celery. Stir into the beans and season generously. Heat the cream in the frying pan, then stir into the beans.

Mediterranean-style Beans

SERVES 4

250g (8 oz) dried white haricot or navy beans (navy is an American
word meaning the service in which they were most eaten, not the
colour), soaked as described on page 75 then drained
4 tablespoons olive oil
1 onion, peeled
1 clove of garlic, peeled and left whole
2 bay leaves
8 tablespoons thick tomato purée or pasatta
Salt and freshly ground black pepper

Mix all the ingredients, except the seasoning, together in a large earthenware casserole, preferably a fairly tall, narrow one, and cover with cold water 2.5cm (1 inch) above the beans. Don't worry if the mixture looks a bit unpromising at this stage. Cover and cook in a preheated oven, 170°C (325°F) gas mark 3, for 2 hours. Stir gently and season to taste. You will find that the liquid has been absorbed by the beans, the onion and garlic have floated to the top, and the whole mixture is fragrant and ready for eating.

The onion and garlic can be discarded or chopped up and stirred back into the beans – their flavour will already have been fully absorbed.

/ CRAFTY TIP /

Soak dried beans in cold water for at least 6 hours, or
overnight if possible. Drain, cover with fresh cold
water and bring to the boil. Boil hard for 10 minutes
before cooking as instructed. This helps to reduce
their gaseous effect!

Pasta

Both the Italians and Chinese have remarkably similar sorts of dishes involving pasta. This is probably because the Italians seem to have borrowed the idea, thanks to Mr M. Polo, from the Chinese around the beginning of the fourteenth century, although there are claims that a similar kind of wheat-based dish to spaghetti was being eaten in Italy in Roman times.

What is certain is that the varieties of pasta that are now available, both hard (dry) and fresh (soft), are remarkable, and serve different purposes. The runnier the sauce you're going to use, the more shaped you need your pasta to be because it will hold the sauce better. Therefore, the ones that look like little snails or bows hold a lot more thin sauce than does long spaghetti or tagliatelle.

Fresh pasta cooks in about a quarter of the time that dry pasta does, although it's not obtainable in so many shapes. It needs just 3 minutes boiling in plenty of fresh water and 1 minute standing. There is a 'crafty' way of cooking dry pasta (that's not been pre-cooked) which makes life much easier – see below.

I've only suggested my four favourite pasta sauces, all of which are European in origin, plus a taste of China.

Crafty Pasta

SERVES 4–6
1 tablespoon oil
Pinch of salt
500g (1 lb) dry pasta

Bring 2.25 litres (4 pints) water to a rolling boil in a very large saucepan. Add the oil, salt and pasta and give it a good stir. Boil for just 3 minutes, remove from the heat, cover and leave for 7 minutes for thick pasta, 5 minutes for thin. Drain and pour over a cupful of cold water. You will find it's cooked absolutely perfectly, without the problem of watching it as closely as you might have to otherwise.

A minute or two longer standing won't hurt it, although it will soften a bit more and stop it being *al dente*, which is how purist Italians like it. You will find the pasta won't stick together, or to the saucepan, and that the water will be almost clear, meaning that very little of the nutritional value has been washed away.

Now add your chosen sauce.

Carbonara Sauce

This is supposedly named after the Italian miners' favourite way of eating pasta. I think it's just a delicious and very simple way of cooking a sauce.

SERVES 4–6

175g (6 oz) salami, cut into matchstick pieces
500g (1 lb) pasta (preferably tagliatelle or thick spaghetti), cooked as on
  page 78 and drained
2 eggs
2 tablespoons double cream (optional)
125g (4 oz) Parmesan cheese, grated

Fry the salami quickly in its own fat until fairly crisp. Place the pasta in a warm bowl. Beat the eggs with the cream, if using, and add to the pasta, stirring quickly. The heat from the pasta will scramble and cook the eggs. Add the salami and Parmesan, mix well and serve at once.

Napolitana Sauce with Courgettes and Mushrooms

This is an adaptation of the classic Neapolitan Tomato Sauce for spaghetti. It is also very nice eaten with any of the long flat noodles that are widely available – red, green or golden.

SERVES 4–6

2 tablespoons olive oil
1 clove of garlic, crushed
175g (6 oz) each courgettes and mushrooms, thinly sliced
1 teaspoon each chopped thyme, oregano and basil
300ml (½ pint) pasatta
500g (1 lb) pasta, cooked as on page 78 and drained
Salt and freshly ground black pepper
Parmesan cheese to serve

Heat the oil in a pan and fry the garlic gently, without browning. Add the courgettes, mushrooms and herbs and season generously. Cook, turning, for 1 minute, then add the pasatta and simmer for at least 5 and not more than 15 minutes. Mix thoroughly with the pasta and serve in bowls, with plenty of Parmesan.

Gorgonzola Sauce

This sauce is incredibly quick and easy and can be made from storecupboard ingredients.

SERVES 4–6

250g (8 oz) Gorgonzola or other creamy blue cheese
4 tablespoons single cream
25g (1 oz) butter
500g (1 lb) pasta (snails or bows are best for this), cooked as on page 78
   and drained
1 tablespoon grated Parmesan cheese

Mash the Gorgonzola with the cream. Melt the butter and add the Gorgonzola, stirring well until it's hot and bubbling. Mix with the pasta in a serving bowl and sprinkle with the Parmesan. Don't be tempted to add more Parmesan as it will destroy the blue cheese taste. Serve at once.

Pasta Primavera

Despite the Italian name of this dish, it was invented and taught to me by a Welsh lady – namely my mother – as a marvellous Sunday lunch dish for people who don't eat meat. Few will notice its absence in the amazing range of textures and flavours this very simple dish provides.

SERVES 4

250g (8 oz) each cauliflower, courgettes, broccoli, green beans and peas
25g (1 oz) butter
250g (8 oz) macaroni or pasta shells, cooked as on page 78 and drained
1 tablespoon chopped parsley
150ml (¼ pint) double cream
2 tablespoons grated Parmesan cheese

Break the cauliflower into florets and cut the courgettes into 1cm (½ inch) slices. Cook all the vegetables together in boiling water for just 5 minutes. Drain well. (If the peas are frozen, leave them out of this part of the exercise.)

   Melt the butter in a large frying pan and fry the drained vegetables, adding frozen peas last. Cook for 3–4 minutes, then place in a serving bowl with the pasta, parsley and cream. Stir thoroughly. Sprinkle with the Parmesan cheese just before serving.

Hot Chinese Salad

Although this is called a salad, it's really a combination dish – various ingredients prepared separately and combined at the last minute. It makes a very good, light vegetarian meal.

SERVES 4

1 tablespoon oil
250g (8 oz) beansprouts
250g (8 oz) green peppers, cored, seeded and sliced into thin rounds
1 bunch of spring onions, chopped
4 sticks of celery, cut into 5mm (1/4 inch) slices
*250g (8 oz) wheat noodles or spaghetti, cooked as on page 78 and
     drained*

FOR THE DRESSING:

4 tablespoons soy sauce
1 tablespoon cider vinegar
2 tablespoons water
1 tablespoon salad oil (sesame oil if possible)
1 teaspoon sugar
1 teaspoon chili sauce

Heat the oil in a wok or deep frying pan and stir fry the beansprouts, peppers, spring onions and celery for 1½ minutes. Place in a serving bowl with the noodles and mix well.

Place the dressing ingredients in a screw-top jar and shake well, or whisk in a bowl. Pour over the hot noodles and vegetables and serve at once.

Vegetarian Lasagne

Lasagne was traditionally a pasta pie, made with a variety of ingredients, the main ones being a red and a white sauce. In fact, its origins in the countryside go back even further, to a time when it was often made with game and other totally unexpected ingredients. Although it's not a strong tradition in Italy, this one leaves out all the meat but none of the flavour.

SERVES 4
500g (1 lb) green lasagne
1 cauliflower, broken into florets
125g (4 oz) strong cheese, grated

RED SAUCE:
2 tablespoons oil
1 large onion, chopped
Small can tomato purée
500g (1 lb) courgettes, sliced
250g (8 oz) mushrooms
1 teaspoon each chopped basil and oregano
1 teaspoon garlic salt
Salt and freshly ground black pepper

WHITE SAUCE:
300ml (½ pint) milk
1 tablespoon each butter and flour

Soak the lasagne in hot water for 10 minutes. (Do not bother to boil, the hot water soaking works quite as well.) Drain and dry it.

To make the red sauce, heat the oil in a pan and fry the onion until softened. Add the tomato purée and an equal quantity of water (that is, fill the empty can) and stir. Season generously, add the courgettes, mushrooms, herbs and garlic salt and simmer while making the white sauce.

Whisk the milk, butter and flour together, then heat steadily, whisking from time to time until thickened.

Take a large, flat baking dish or gratin dish at least 3.5cm (1½ inches) deep. Put some white sauce in the bottom and add the cauliflower florets. Cover with half the lasagne, then the red sauce. Cover with the remaining lasagne, then the remaining white sauce. Sprinkle the cheese over the top. Cook in a preheated oven, 180°C (350°F) gas mark 4, for 45 minutes, until bubbling and golden.

Something Fishy

The first two recipes in this chapter illustrate the development in cooking over the last fifteen years in this country. At first glance they may look very similar: both being cod steaks in a creamy sauce with mushrooms. In fact, they are the *same* recipe, first in the original Capital Radio form then the latest television version. Both are crafty and taste good, but the modern one uses fresh *not* frozen or canned ingredients. That may seem like a small change, but it demonstrates one of the dominant concerns of most of us today – the possible effect of food on our health.

Yes – food has become a leisure pursuit; yes – we have learned to enjoy new tastes and exotic flavours; yes – we have rediscovered some pride in our own cooking. But one factor unites the old-age pensioner studying the label on a can of fruit in a supermarket where I was filming and Raymond Blanc shopping for his expensive top *Good Food Guide* restaurant. It is concern about the ingredients. Are they additive free? No preservatives? Even, in the case of fruit and vegetables, a hope that they are organically grown.

Fish, of course, answers a lot of health questions more easily than most foods. With the occasional exception of some shellfish and the new supplies of farmed salmon and trout, fish are caught wild, and the worst that usually happens to them is the addition of extra water as they are frozen. I think it's that aspect, together with the lightness of even rich fish dishes, that accounts for their recent surge in popularity. And a surge it has been. A few years ago my notes show I was describing monkfish as a good alternative to lobster, and cheaper than cod. Not any more on the price front! It's still a firm succulent fish with practically no bones and waste, but not cheap. It's been discovered, along with a whole lot more of our traditional piscine species . . . the recently re-established herring, for instance.

The fresher fish is, the less it needs done to it. A truly fresh sole takes some beating, when it is skinned, grilled and served with a pat of butter mixed with a spoonful each of parsley and lemon juice. So too does a freshly caught, baked mackerel, eaten with the simplest gooseberry sauce. But even with the sudden sprouting of fresh-fish counters at supermarkets, none of us can always guarantee fabulously fresh flounder. So here is a selection of traditional and modern ideas for the fish you should be able to acquire without your own rod and line. If you do happen to catch the big one, the Saumon Vert recipe is the one for you!

Cod in Mushroom Sauce

SERVES 4
4 cod steaks (frozen)
175 g (6 oz) button mushrooms, sliced
1 can condensed mushroom soup
5 tablespoons double cream (optional)

Place the cod steaks in a buttered baking dish and scatter the mushrooms over the top. Stir the soup and pour into the dish, together with the cream – if you're feeling extravagant. Bake in a preheated oven, 170°C (325°F) gas mark 3, for 40 minutes. Serve with buttered new potatoes and French beans.

Cod and Mushrooms in Soured Cream

Soured cream in much undervalued in Britain. It's much lower in fat than double cream and has a richness just tempered by the careful souring. Fresh cream that has gone off is not the same thing! This recipe is a great dish if you have an oven with a timer. If everything is cool when assembled, it can be left for up to 4 hours, ready to cook.

SERVES 4
4 cod steaks, boned
2 tablespoons oil
250g (8 oz) button mushrooms, sliced
150ml (1/4 pint) soured cream
Juice and grated rind of 1 lemon

Put the cod steaks in a buttered baking dish. Heat the oil in a pan and sauté the mushrooms for 3 minutes. Leave to cool.

Beat the soured cream, lemon juice and rind together, stir in the mushrooms and pour over the cod steaks, making sure they are completely coated.

Cover with foil and cook in a preheated oven, 200°C (400°F) gas mark 6, for 25 minutes. Take the foil off for the last 5 minutes to allow the sauce to brown a little. This is very good served with peas and lots of mashed potato.

Shrimps New Orleans

In Louisiana they have shrimps the size of our baby lobsters, but even our smaller cousins can come up trumps in the spicy sauce from the Queen of Southern American Cities. The tropical bean-like okra gives the sauce a slightly gelatinous texture that's called a 'gumbo' in New Orleans.

SERVES 4

2 tablespoons vegetable oil
1 clove of garlic, chopped
1 Spanish onion, chopped
1 each red and green pepper, cored, seeded and chopped
250g (8 oz) okra, cut into 5mm (¼ inch) lengths
250g (8 oz) can tomatoes
½ teaspoon each allspice and cayenne pepper
500g (1 lb) shrimps, peeled (the bigger the better)
Salt and freshly ground black pepper

Heat the oil and fry the garlic for 1 minute. Add the onion, peppers and okra and fry for 5 minutes, then add the tomatoes and cook for 25 minutes. Season to taste, add the spices and shrimps and cook for just 3 minutes – they can become rubbery if you cook them much longer. Serve with boiled rice, followed by a salad.

Monkfish Almondine

SERVES 4

750g (1½ lb) monkfish
300ml (½ pint) apple juice
1 bay leaf
150ml (¼ pint) single cream
25g (1 oz) butter
1 tablespoon flour
50g (2 oz) ground almonds
1 tablespoon lemon juice
75g (3 oz) cheese (preferably Gruyère), grated
1 teaspoon salt
Freshly ground black pepper

Place the fish in a shallow oval dish, pour over the apple juice and add the bay leaf. Cover and cook in a preheated oven, 180°C (350°F) gas mark 4, for 20 minutes. Drain off the liquid into a small pan. Keep the fish warm.

Add the cream, butter and flour to the cooling liquid and cook, whisking, until it thickens. Add the almonds, lemon juice, cheese and seasoning, stir and pour over the fish. Place under a hot grill until the top is brown and bubbly. Serve with mashed potato and broccoli or beans.

Monkfish with Three-star Sauce

This sauce is an adaptation of the green peppercorn sauce, one of the classic dishes of *nouvelle cuisine*. I've copied it from a great chef called Michel Guérard who adds finely chopped red peppers to make a sauce that's prettier and tastier than the original. Monkfish has the strength and texture to survive this vigorous saucing unbowed, whereas other fish might have succumbed and adopted 'background' status.

SERVES 4
750g (1½ lb) monkfish
50g (2 oz) butter
300ml (½ pint) water
½ red pepper, cored, seeded and finely chopped
1 tablespoon green peppercorns
150ml (¼ pint) double cream
1 tablespoon lemon juice
Salt

Cut the monkfish across the grain into rounds. Melt the butter in a large pan, carefully pour in the water and stir to mix. Add the fish, cover and cook for 15 minutes until tender, without allowing the water to reach a vigorous boil. Discard the liquid and add the red pepper and peppercorns to the pan. Pour in the cream, add the lemon juice and gently bring to the boil, spooning the sauce over the fish. Simmer for 1 minute and season with salt only to taste. Serve with rice and a delicate green vegetable like mangetouts.

Monkfish Kebabs

The three secrets with any kebab are to use flat skewers (so that turning the kebab is easy), to use a fierce heat (so that the food seals quickly on the outside), and to use ingredients which provide a variety of texture and colour. I think this combination of monkfish and spices with a slightly 'eastern' flavour is perfect.

SERVES 4

1 clove of garlic, crushed
150g (5 oz) plain yoghurt
1 dessertspoon mild *curry powder*
750g (1½ lb) monkfish , cut into cubes
1 each red and green pepper, cored, seeded and cut into 2.5cm (1 inch)
squares

Mix together the garlic, yoghurt and curry powder in a bowl. Add the fish and marinate for at least 4 hours.

Thread the fish and pepper slices alternately onto flat skewers, beginning and ending with pepper. Press the fish fairly tightly together so that it forms a unit with the peppers. Cook under a really hot grill for about 5 minutes on each side, basting occasionally with the marinade, until the fish is brown and sizzling all over.

Serve on a bed of pilau rice with chutneys and poppadoms and, if you like it, a little more yoghurt mixed into a cucumber salad.

CRAFTY TIP

When buying fish, ask the fishmonger to give you all the trimmings (and other people's if they don't want them). Use them to make fish soup (see page 32).

Mediterranean Fish Casserole

Rich, aromatic and spicy, this dish is not for the timid! It's not that it's difficult to cook, but it should really be kept for your special friends – those whose happiest memories are of a little candle-lit taverna on some sun-kissed Greek isle, where the scent of rosemary wafts on the breeze and the scent of garlic on the steam from the kitchen.

SERVES 6–8

4 tablespoons vegetable oil
250g (8 oz) onions, finely chopped
3 cloves of garlic, crushed
400g (14 oz) can tomatoes
500g (1 lb) squid, preferably small
500g (1 lb) grey mullet, skinned and filleted
600ml (1 pint) mussels, prepared as described on page 92
½ teaspoon chili powder
1 teaspoon each dried basil and oregano
125g (4 oz) prawns, peeled
Salt and freshly ground black pepper

Heat the oil in a pan and fry the onion and garlic for 5 minutes, until golden. Add the tomatoes, cover and simmer for 15 minutes. Stir until smooth.

Meanwhile, clean the squid. Wash them under cold running water – the purple skin just peels off. Take out all the insides and discard (including the transparent quill). You can keep the tentacles, but pull out the hard 'beak' in the middle.

Cut the squid into rings and the mullet into 2.5cm (1 inch) cubes and add to the sauce with the mussels. Add the chili powder, herbs and seasoning to taste and simmer for just 5 minutes. Add the prawns and simmer for 1 minute. Discard any mussels that have not opened.

Serve in bowls with rice or – best of all – crusty bread.

Rich Fish Pie

For too many of us fish pie is a school horror story. If that's true for you, this version should cure any nightmarish memories. The only problem with it is that you really need a second one waiting in the oven after the first round has been demolished. Try it – it'll keep very well in the freezer if their eyes turn out to be bigger than their tummies.

SERVES 4

500g (1 lb) white fish – cod, coley or whiting fillet
1 onion, chopped
300 ml (½ pint) water and milk mixed
2 tablespoons flour
25g (1 oz) butter
125g (4 oz) button mushrooms
125g (4 oz) packet frozen mixed fancy vegetables, including peppers
   and sweetcorn
125g (4 oz) shrimps, peeled
4 hard-boiled eggs, quartered
500g (1 lb) warm mashed potato
1 egg, beaten
Salt and freshly ground black pepper

Place the fish, onion and milk and water in a saucepan, cover and cook gently for about 8 minutes. Remove the fish and flake into big pieces.

Whisk the flour and butter into the cooking liquid. Bring slowly to the boil, whisking occasionally, until thickened. Add the mushrooms and vegetables and simmer for 2 minutes. Mix in the fish and shrimps and season lightly to taste. Transfer to an oval pie dish and add the eggs. Cover with the potato, brush with beaten egg and bake in a preheated oven, 190°C (375°F) gas mark 5, for 25 minutes.

CRAFTY TIP

To skin fish, it should be filleted first, except for sole. Place it, skin down, tail towards you. Put some table salt on your fingers, seize the tail end and, with a sharp knife tilted a little downwards, cut away from you parallel to the work top. The skin will peel off quite easily.

Sole Veronique

Fish and grapes may seem a bit unexpected at first, but this is one of France's classic fish dishes. It's not that surprising really: remember our own mackerel and gooseberries. The combination is delicious, especially if you use the muscatel grapes you can buy in the late summer. Give it a try – you'll be surprised by the balance of flavours.

SERVES 4

2 soles, filleted and skinned (lemon are okay, Dover are best)
300ml (½ pint) white grape juice
Juice of 1 lemon
150ml (¼ pint) double cream
1 teaspoon flour
7g (¼ oz) butter
125g (4 oz) white grapes, halved and seeded
Salt and freshly ground black pepper

Put the sole fillets in a baking dish, season to taste and cover with the grape and lemon juices. Cover with buttered foil and cook in a preheated oven, 190°C (375°F) gas mark 5, for 15 minutes, until the fish is just cooked. Strain the juices into a pan and add the cream. Whisk in the flour and butter, then whisk the mixture over heat until thick and smooth. Season to taste with salt and freshly ground black pepper.

Place the grapes on or around the fillets, pour over the sauce and return to the oven for 5 minutes. This dish is good served with new potatoes and a crisp green salad.

Haddock Dieppoise

This is how fish is served in the restaurants along the quay at Dieppe. If you are travelling across to France and have the luck to land in Dieppe, make sure you allow yourself time for lunch. The seafood in the restaurants there is really terrific and has the richness of Normandy cooking, combined with the freshness of the sea. This is a classic recipe from that area, combining white fish, shellfish, mushrooms and a Normandy cream sauce – a wonderful combination set off by a quick glazing under the grill.

SERVES 4

500g (1 lb) haddock, boned and skinned
150ml (¼ pint) white wine or white grape juice
1 tablespoon cornflour
25g (1 oz) butter
150ml (¼ pint) single cream
125g (4 oz) button mushrooms
125g (4 oz) shrimps, peeled
Salt and freshly ground black pepper

Divide the fish in half and place in a buttered heatproof dish. Pour in the wine or grape juice and season to taste. Cover and cook in a preheated oven, 180°C (350°F) gas mark 4, for 20 minutes.

Pour the liquid into a pan. Whisk together the cornflour, butter and cream. Add to the pan and bring to the boil, whisking, until smooth. Add the mushrooms, shrimps and season to taste. Pour over the fish and place under a hot grill for 1 minute, to glaze. Serve at once.

Cod Portuguese

From further south than Normandy comes a different way of cooking white fish. Even the Portuguese admit that almost every dish they make has tomatoes and onions in it – this one's no exception. In fact, the tomato and onion mixture is so well known that the French call anything where the sauce is dominated by those two ingredients 'Portuguese'. It's still a delicious recipe, very simple to make, and gives a nice exotic flavour to cod.

SERVES 4

6 tablespoons olive oil
1 Spanish onion, sliced
500g (1 lb) potatoes, boiled for 8 minutes then sliced
500g (1 lb) can tomatoes
4 cod steaks, skinned and boned if possible
Salt and freshly ground black pepper

Heat 4 tablespoons of the oil in a pan and fry the onion very gently for 15 minutes. Fry the potatoes in the remaining oil in a separate pan at the same time. Add the tomatoes to the onion and boil for 5 minutes. Add the fish to the tomato and onion mixture and simmer for about 7 minutes, spooning the sauce over. Stir in the potatoes, season to taste, cover and cook for 5 minutes. Serve with a salad.

Mussels

Mussels are the most under-rated of all our shellfish. They're still remarkably cheap and, with the new pre-cleaned versions that come from Ireland and North Wales, most of your work is already done for you. The really boring thing with mussels used to be scraping and scrubbing the shells, but now all you have to do is make sure that the beards are completely removed and the mussels are totally closed before you consider cooking them. Check by banging them with the back of a knife – if they don't close within a minute, discard them.

Even if they are cleaned, wash the mussels carefully in cold water, then let them stand for 30 minutes in clean water with a pinch of salt. Discard any that are cracked or open and scrape the beardy bits off all the good ones with a sharp knife. They are now ready to use.

The following three very simple dishes can all be made from one large bag (3 quarts, which is roughly equivalent to 2 kilos) of mussels. Each will serve 4 people.

Moules Marinière

Place 1 quart of mussels in a heavy-based pan containing 2.5cm (1 inch) depth of water, a finely chopped onion and a pinch of salt. Cover, bring to the boil and keep at boiling point for 5 minutes, shaking the pan occasionally. The mussels will steam open. Remove them, throwing away any unopened ones, and place in a big tureen or bowl. Sprinkle with a handful of chopped parsley and 1 teaspoon salt, then pour over the strained cooking liquid. Serve with plenty of hot French bread and butter.

Mussels Normande

Cook another quart in the same way, substituting apple juice for the water and leaving out the onion. Pull off each mussel's loose half shell before putting them in the bowl. Sprinkle with parsley and salt as above. Mix 150ml (¼ pint) double cream with the cooking liquid and pour over the mussels. This makes a very grand first course for a dinner party.

Breton Mussels

Cook the third quart like the first. When cooked, remove the mussels from their shells and thread on skewers, alternating with button mushrooms and 2.5cm (1 inch) pieces of lightly fried chipolata sausages. Brush with oil and grill for 3 minutes. Serve with rice and a salad as a main course.

Koulibiaca

This is a splendid Russian recipe for fish in pastry. I always use frozen puff pastry because making fresh seems a real burden. Now that there are vegetarian puff pastries available everywhere, you can buy ready-made without the worry of huge amounts of animal fat. Made with salmon, Koulibiaca is quite a posh dish, regarded as a part of *haute cuisine*, but I like it best made with one of the smoked fishes in fairly hefty chunks.

SERVES 4

500g (1 lb) smoked cod or coley
450ml (¾ pint) milk and water mixed
1 onion, chopped
175g (6 oz) long grain rice
150ml (¼ pint) soured cream
250g (8 oz) frozen puff pastry, thawed
Milk for brushing

Place the fish, milk and water in a pan, cover and cook gently for 10 minutes. Remove the fish from the pan and set aside to cool.

Add the onion and rice to the cooking liquid and cook gently for 12 minutes, then drain. Mix the onion and rice with the soured cream.

Roll out the pastry to a rectangle and mark horizontally across the centre. Place the fish in the middle of one half and cover with the rice and onion, leaving a 2.5cm (1 inch) border around the edges. Fold the pastry over, seal the edges and brush with milk. Bake in a preheated oven, 200°C (400°F) gas mark 6, for 20 minutes.

Serve with French beans or a salad of chicory and orange slices.

Fish Cakes

The commercial version has spoiled us for good fish cakes, but there are many versions from all over the world that are well worth making: light flaky New England crab cakes, the spicy solid fish cakes from south-east Asia and this version from north of our border, using a mixture of smoked and fresh fish. The classic recipe uses fresh and smoked haddock, but most smoked fish, even the cheaper whiting, makes a lovely combination of flavours.

SERVES 4

250g (8 oz) white fish – cod, whiting or haddock
250g (8 oz) smoked golden fish – haddock or golden cutlets
300ml (½ pint) milk
Ground nutmeg
500g (1 lb) potatoes, boiled
25g (1 oz) butter
1 egg, beaten
2 heaped tablespoons soft breadcrumbs (not the hard golden type you
    buy in packets)

Place the fish, milk and a pinch of nutmeg in a pan, cover and cook gently for about 10 minutes. Skin, bone and flake the fish, reserving the milk.

Mash the potatoes with ½ teaspoon nutmeg, the butter and reserved milk. Add the fish and mix to a smooth consistency. Divide into 8 balls and shape into cakes. Allow to cool. Dip into the egg, then the breadcrumbs, pressing them in firmly. Chill for at least 1 hour before frying.

They will keep for up to 3 or 4 days before cooking if kept at a low enough temperature, but not frozen.

Saumon Vert

There are many recipes for cut-up salmon which, like trout, is now extensively farmed and widely available. There are few things as nice as a plain grilled salmon steak with a little knob of melted lemon-flavoured butter over the top and a good pinch of parsley, eaten with new potatoes and a cucumber salad. But however delicious cut-up salmon may be, there is nothing like the 'king of the sea' in one piece. This recipe is one of the most spectacular of all salmon dishes. It's meant as the centrepiece for a party or a grand buffet, and I've used it with enormous success at celebrations as varied as a bat mitzvah and my own daughter's wedding.

SERVES 8

1 whole salmon, weighing 1.75–2.25kg (4–5 lb) (or more if you're
  feeling rich!)
2 lemons
A bouquet garni (celery, thyme and parsley sprig, tied together)
1 tablespoon black peppercorns
2 cucumbers

FOR THE MAYONNAISE:

4 eggs
300ml (½ pint) each olive and sunflower oil
6 tablespoons lemon juice
2 tablespoons Dijon mustard
4 teaspoons salt
4 teaspoons sugar
Freshly ground black pepper

Place the fish in a large fish kettle or wrap it carefully in well buttered foil.

If using a fish kettle, cover the salmon with cold water, add the juice of the lemons, bouquet garni and peppercorns and bring to the boil. Simmer for 4 minutes only, then cover, turn off the heat and leave to cool in its own liquid. Surprisingly, it will cook through in this time.

If using foil, slice the lemons and lay them on both sides of the fish, squeezing over the juice from the ends. Seal the foil carefully without pressing it down on to the fish, place in a large ovenproof dish and cook in a preheated oven, 180°C (350°F) gas mark 4, for 10 minutes per 500g (1 lb). Remove from the oven and allow to cool without opening the foil.

When the fish is cold, skin it very carefully (the skin should come away without any difficulty), remove the fins and lay it on a serving dish. Score the cucumbers lengthways with a fork and then slice very thinly. Lay the slices on the fish, starting at the head, overlapping them to recreate fish scales. The frilly effect on the edge of the cucumber makes a marvellous pattern. Arrange the rest of the cucumber in overlapping rows around the dish, both to decorate it and to be eaten later.

Make the mayonnaise, as described on page 27, using half the ingredients at a time. Serve separately.

Poultry and Game

Henri IV of France occupies a similar position in the public's affection across the Channel as his namesake Henry VIII does in England. And if our Good King Hal's reputation was more for gourmand than gourmet food, Henri IV has equivalent claim to culinary fame. His political reputation was built on the avowed aim of a chicken in every pot, every Sunday.

Until recently, well within my cooking lifetime, chicken was a luxury to be looked forward to on Sundays. By 1986 the pattern had reached the other extreme, with chicken becoming the cheapest and most common raw meat we bought in Britain. Up to then, beef had reigned supreme. Various kinds of accelerated production have meant chicken has become an everyday dish, though many people think that this has been at the expense of flavour, texture and even humanity.

As to the argument about the flavour of today's chickens, one of the central problems is that of the super-efficiency of the modern chicken industry. However they have been raised, unless you buy your chicken from a butcher who specialises in having meat that's aged properly, your chicken was probably killed, cleaned and chilled within an hour. If it was also frozen, it will have had little time at all to develop any flavour. This doesn't mean that chicken should be hung like game, but there is no question that a little ageing allows the slightly metallic, newly-killed flavour that's often commented on with modern broiler chickens to mellow and go away. It's also worth remembering, though our modern high-speed society doesn't make much allowance for it, that boiling chickens have more flavour and a great deal more texture than roasters.

A good trick, if you're looking for improved flavour and texture, is to allow a chicken that's been frozen or chilled to 'mature' in a cool fridge for at least 24 hours, with the wrappings off and the giblets removed from the cavity. This will produce a remarkable improvement in both the taste and texture of your finished dish.

Over the years, crafty cooking has always regarded chicken as the most important of meats. The parallel interests in healthier eating, lighter food and more intensely flavoured sauces have all brought chicken to the centre of the stage, as a dish in its own right or merely as a base. Now, more than ever, the demand for chicken has created a need for an even greater variety of chicken recipes.

Recent nutritional research suggests than non-feathered game (rabbit, hare, venison) is also some of the best red meat you can eat – low in fat, almost certainly no additives and rich enough in flavour and texture to make a moderate amount very filling. I have included three very basic recipes to introduce you to what's often regarded with a certain amount of trepidation by most cooks. They are all very crafty recipes and, although they follow the principles of their originals, are really very simple to achieve.

Chicken Stock

There is no comparison between home-made stock and that made with stock cubes. The former makes superb soups and really 'lifts' casseroles. It's not difficult to make, either. For the basis, use a carcass left from a roast chicken, or all the odd bits left after jointing a chicken, plus the giblets.

MAKES 1.2 LITRES (2 PINTS)
1 chicken carcass, or the back, wing tips and leg bits left after jointing
Giblets (except liver)
1.2 litres (2 pints) water
1 bay leaf
1 teaspoon salt
Pinch of cinnamon
Slice of lemon

Rinse the chicken pieces if using a jointed bird. Place in a large saucepan, with the giblets, cover with the water and bring to the boil. Skim the surface to remove scummy bits, then add the other ingredients. Simmer for 1 hour.

Strain the stock into a basin or jug and use as required for soups and casseroles. If you don't want to use it at once, place in the refrigerator. When thoroughly cold, remove the fat that will have settled on the surface. You can then keep it for about 3 days in the fridge, or freeze it in usable quantities for later use.

CRAFTY TIP

Never throw away a chicken carcass, trimmings or giblets when you've eaten the roast chicken – use them to make stock (see page 97). You will be really surprised at the difference it makes to recipes. You don't have to use it straight away either, as it freezes very well for up to 3 months. If you freeze it in the amounts you most often use, you will always have it ready to hand. You can even use it straight from the freezer – simply melt it over heat before adding to the dish.

The Crafty Roast Chicken

This is my favourite chicken recipe of all time – it's also the one most favoured by my family. It's a very simple way of roasting a chicken, a task that may seem to need no instruction, but this technique produces a delicately flavoured bird that's moist and delicious, with a crisp skin and succulent flesh, whether it's eaten hot with a cream sauce or cold with salad. It can also be used for chicken portions – simply reduce the cooking time.

This recipe follows an early crafty tradition, by the way, of using garlic salt. While I use it a great deal less than I used to, on this occasion it's quite the best and simplest way of achieving the flavour.

SERVES 4–6
1 × 1.5–1.75 kg (3½–4 lb) roasting chicken
1 teaspoon each garlic salt, powdered bay leaves and paprika
½ a lemon
Freshly ground black pepper

Make sure the chicken is at room temperature. Remove all the giblets and any surplus fat from the cavity. Squeeze the lemon over the whole chicken, then place the squeezed half inside the cavity. Sprinkle the garlic salt, bay leaves and paprika over the top, sides and legs of the chicken, putting a small pinch inside the cavity on each occasion, and season with pepper to taste. Place in a baking dish into which it just fits comfortably. Cover with 1 or 2 used butter papers (with some butter still sticking to them) or lightly butter a piece of foil and lay it over the top of the chicken. The intention is not to wrap the chicken in the paper or foil, but merely to keep it moist and basted with butter during its cooking.

Cook in a preheated oven, 190°C (375°F) gas mark 5, for about 45 minutes. Remove the paper or foil for the last 15 minutes – it will have browned pretty thoroughly underneath it anyway. Allow the chicken to stand for 5 minutes after you take it out of the oven to reabsorb its juices. The total cooking time should be, depending on the size of the chicken, about 1 hour. If you want to eat it just as it is, carve it, remove the surplus fat from the juices in the dish and use for gravy.

If you prefer a fancier method of serving, cut it into joints and place on a serving dish. Heat the juices in the pan with 2 tablespoons cream mixed with 1 dessertspoon cornflour and about half a cup of water. This will produce a wonderful herby, garlicky cream sauce to pour over the chicken.

If you want to eat it cold, allow it to cool under the butter papers, in the pan it was cooked in, before putting it in the fridge. You will find that it will remain moist and flavoursome for 24 hours without needing to be wrapped in foil or clingfilm. It's particularly nice in the summer, cut into portions and served with a salad that includes some fruit, particularly white grapes.

Tarragon Chicken

A variation of the crafty roast chicken with a distinctly French flavour.

SERVES 4–6
1 × 1.5–1.75kg (3½–4 lb) roasting chicken
25g (1 oz) butter
1 tablespoon chopped tarragon or 1 teaspoon dried
1 clove of garlic
1 teaspoon salt
1 lemon

Clean and prepare the chicken as above. Butter the breast, wings and legs lightly with a knife, as though it were bread, then sprinkle with the tarragon. Crush the garlic with the salt and place half inside the cavity of the chicken and the other half under the chicken. Squeeze half the lemon over the chicken and add the unsqueezed half to the cavity. Cover lightly with foil and cook as above.

Thicken the juices as above to make a sauce very strongly flavoured with tarragon and lemon.

Chicken Pieces

Here are three recipes, all using the same basic method for cooking chicken pieces, and all with cream sauces. They come from every period of crafty cooking and some have more classic origins than others. They are delicious and are surprisingly different, despite the similarity of technique.

Chicken with Asparagus

The French have a name for a boneless piece of chicken cut from the breast. They call it the *suprême*, and I think that, teamed with asparagus, this is really chicken with class! If you wish to cook six breasts, use the larger quantities where given.

SERVES 4 OR 6
1 tablespoon vegetable oil
25–40g (1–1½ oz) butter
4 or 6 breasts of chicken, boned
150–250ml (5–8 fl oz) water
1–1½ tablespoons flour
150–250ml (5–8 fl oz) double cream
250g (8 oz) packet frozen asparagus, thawed (or a can will do)
½–¾ teaspoon salt
Freshly ground black pepper

Heat the oil and butter together in a large pan and fry the chicken for 5 minutes. Add the water, cover and cook gently for about 15 minutes. Remove the chicken and keep warm on a serving dish. Whisk the flour into the liquid, then whisk in the cream. Add the asparagus, reserving a little for garnish, season to taste and heat through until boiling. Pour over the chicken and garnish with the reserved asparagus to serve.

Chicken and Chives

This recipe is the basis for a wide variety of chicken-and-herb-in-cream-sauce dishes, varied according to the herbs you have available. A bunch of chives is very easy to grow, even in a window box, but tarragon, fennel or even parsley all work well. It really is, however, a dish that requires fresh not dried herbs.

SERVES 4

25g (1 oz) butter
4 chicken pieces
175ml (6 fl oz) white grape juice
150ml (5 fl oz) double cream
1 teaspoon cornflour
Approximately 12 strands chives

Melt the butter in a frying pan and fry the chicken for 5 minutes. Add the grape juice, cover and cook for 15 minutes. Blend the cream with the cornflour and add to the pan with the chives. Bring back to the boil and serve immediately.

Chicken Stroganoff

A dish named after a Russian aristocrat of the nineteenth century. At this particular point in Russian history, all things French were terribly fashionable, but the soured cream that crept into this recipe somehow maintains its Slavic origins, in a very distinctive way. It's a dish that has instant likeability and I find it very useful to serve to people who are frightened of 'messed around food' but are willing to experiment a little.

SERVES 4

25g (1 oz) butter
4 chicken pieces
175g (6 oz) button mushrooms, halved or sliced
1 Spanish onion, sliced into rings
150ml (5 fl oz) soured cream

Melt the butter in a frying pan and fry the chicken pieces gently until golden. Add water to a depth of about 2.5cm (1 inch) and simmer for 15 minutes, turning the chicken pieces occasionally. Add the mushrooms and onion and simmer for 5 minutes. Transfer the chicken to a serving dish.

Add the cream to the pan and heat through gently. Pour over the chicken. Serve with buttered shell or bar noodles and sautéed courgettes.

/ **CRAFTY TIP** /

To cut down on your fat intake even more, remove
the skin from chicken pieces before cooking. Simply
snip the skin, lift and pull away from the flesh, then
cut off with kitchen scissors – it's a very quick and
easy task. Cut off any layers of fat beneath the skin, too.

Chicken Simla

The flavours of this dish come from our imperial past – the spendours of the
Raj, tiffin at the club in Simla. But this recipe, though it has eastern promise,
won't sear your oesophagus. It's a lovely combination of spicy and sweet. If
you cook six chicken pieces, use the larger amounts given for the other
ingredients.

SERVES 4 OR 6

1–1½ tablespoons curry powder
1–1½ tablespoons caster sugar
1–1½ teaspoons salt
4– 6 chicken pieces
4– 6 tablespoons mango chutney
3– 4 tablespoons Worcestershire sauce
50–75g (2–3 oz) butter, melted
3– 4 tablespoons lemon juice

Stir together the curry powder, sugar and salt and spoon on to the chicken.
Leave for at least 2 hours.

Line the grill pan with foil and heat the grill for 5 minutes. Grill the
chicken, skin side up, for 10 minutes, turn and grill the other side for 5–8
minutes. Turn it again.

Mix all the other ingredients together and pour carefully over the chicken.
Grill for 10–15 minutes, until bubbling gently.

Serve with rice and a green salad – and be sure to pour all the juices over
the chicken.

Poulet Landaise

This is one of those country chicken casseroles that the French are so good at. It comes from the Landes, the great long stretch of sandy beaches and pine woods that runs from the mouth of the Gironde almost to the Pyrenees. Slightly inland is where some of the best French cooking is supposed to come from, but the Landes itself is the home of a lot of interesting and little known dishes. This casserole appears very simple and is crafty to make, but it has a surprisingly rich and complex taste.

SERVES 4
4 chicken pieces
Flour for coating
4 tablespoons olive oil
1 large onion, finely chopped
2 cloves of garlic, chopped
1 teaspoon each dried thyme, tarragon and basil
4 tablespoons tomato purée
250g (8 oz) ripe tomatoes, very finely chopped
2 red peppers, cored, seeded and very finely chopped
½ teaspoon each sugar, salt and pepper

Toss the chicken pieces in flour until well coated. Heat the oil in a flameproof casserole and sauté the chicken pieces until golden brown all over. Add the onion, garlic and herbs and simmer for 5 minutes. Add the tomato purée, tomatoes and red peppers, stir and add just enough water to cover the chicken – not enough to make it swill about. Cover and cook in a preheated oven, 180°C (350°F) gas mark 4, for 1½ hours. Season with the sugar, salt and pepper and serve with rice. Don't be tempted to serve a vegetable as well – follow the French practice of serving a separate vegetable course afterwards. Something green is ideal after the rich, dark red flavour and colour of this stew.

CRAFTY TIP

If a recipe calls for very finely chopped onions, tomatoes, peppers, mushrooms and so on, use a food processor. It speeds up the job tremendously and really does give you a finely chopped ingredient. Watch it though – a few seconds too long and you could end up with a purée!

Crafty Cok

This is the very crafty version of the traditional French Coq au Vin. When that dish is made well, it can be one of the great dishes of the world. When it's a scraggy roasting fowl washing about in the remains of nasty cheap red wine, it can be absolutely disgusting. This method actually doesn't use wine at all, but the much more economic red grape juice known as Francerre. I find that unless you're prepared to use a really expensive bottle of wine for cooking – one costing more than £5 – you get a much better result with the very intensely flavoured but slightly sweet red grape juice.

As with so many peasant dishes, the actual origins of this one are much in dispute and go back into pre- 'written recipe' periods. This is a simple version and follows the belief that the best French cooking has comparatively few stages, but very good ingredients.

You can tell whether what you're buying is a cockerel because it should be larger than a chicken – at least 2.25kg (5 lb) or even 3.2kg (7 lb) – its skin should be darker and the claws big and bright yellow.

SERVES 4–6
1 boiling chicken, preferably a large cockerel
Flour for coating
1 tablespoon oil
25g (1 oz) butter

2 cloves of garlic, peeled but left whole
½ an onion
1 bottle of Francerre
Bouquet garni consisting of 1 large celery stick with some leaves, 2 bay
*   leaves and 4–5 thick parsley stalks (heads aren't important), tied*
*   together with cotton or in a muslin bag so it can be fished out*
*   efficiently*
Salt and freshly ground black pepper

Cut the chicken up into pieces (or ask your butcher to do it for you) and flour them generously. Heat the oil and butter together in a flameproof casserole and fry the chicken pieces until well browned. Add the cloves of garlic, onion and the Francerre and bring to a fierce boil. Add the bouquet garni, season to taste, cover and simmer for 3 hours, either on top of the stove or in a preheated oven, 150°C (300°F) gas mark 2. Remove the bouquet garni.

If the sauce is not thick enough, thicken with a little cornflour blended with water and a small knob of butter, to give the sauce a shine.

Serve, traditionally, with little triangles of fried bread and boiled new potatoes with parsley. Serve any vegetables as a separate course.

There are very authentic versions of this dish which include button mushrooms and baby onions – plus one or two other ingredients as well on occasion – but I think the simpler the dish, the better the flavour and the richer the sauce.

Mediterranean Chicken

Another French chicken casserole, this time from Provence. It's a one-dish meal – the potatoes are cooked with the olive-flavoured chicken and herbs – perfect for a lazy type of day. My thanks for it to Bob Carrier.

SERVES 4
3 tablespoons vegetable oil
500g (1 lb) potatoes, cut into 1cm (½ inch) cubes
3 cloves of garlic, crushed
1 × 1.3kg (3 lb) chicken
½ teaspoon each dried tarragon and basil
250g (8 oz) tomatoes, skinned and chopped
Black olives (optional)
Salt and freshly ground black pepper

Heat 2 tablespoons of the oil in a heavy metal casserole dish and fry the potatoes for 10 minutes. Remove and set aside. Add the rest of the oil, the garlic and the whole chicken and cook for about 10 minutes, turning the chicken until browned all over. Add the herbs and tomatoes, season to taste, cover and simmer very gently for 40 minutes. Don't let it burn – add a little water if it starts to.

Add the potatoes and black olives, if you like them, increase the heat and cook, uncovered, for about 10 minutes, until the potatoes are properly cooked, stirring them frequently. Serve with a tossed green salad.

CRAFTY TIP

To test if chicken is cooked – whether it's roasted, fried, grilled or casseroled – pierce the thigh with a skewer. If the juices run clear, it's cooked. If there's a hint of pink, it's not. Use the same test for roast turkey and duck.

Southern Fried Chicken

This is the recipe that reveals Colonel Sanders' secret. Southern-style fried chicken is succulent because of the steam 'pressure' cooking it has towards the end. Contrary to popular belief, it's shallow-fried, not deep-fried. Give 'em a taste of this and they'll all be singing Dixie!

SERVES 4
4 chicken pieces
3 tablespoons flour
1 tablespoon ground cinnamon
1 teaspoon garlic salt
1 egg, beaten
600ml (1 pint) vegetable oil (approximately)
300ml (½ pint) milk

Cut each chicken portion in half and dust with the flour mixed with the cinnamon and garlic salt. Dip each piece in beaten egg and coat again with the flour mixture.

Heat about 5mm–1cm (¼–½ inch) depth of oil in a wide frying pan and fry the chicken quickly on both sides to seal it, then – and this is the secret of

Southern fried chicken – lower the heat and cover the pan. This will make the chicken crisp on the outside and steamed on the inside. Cook for 15 minutes, removing the lid for the last 5 minutes to crisp it up well. Transfer to a serving dish and keep warm.

To make the gravy, pour almost all the oil out of the pan, add the surplus flour mixture and fry for 1 minute. Stir in the milk, bring to the boil and cook for 2–3 minutes. This will make a thick creamy-coloured gravy to serve with the chicken. Mashed potatoes, sweetcorn and fried bananas are the traditional accompaniments.

CRAFTY TIP

To improve flavour and texture in frozen or chilled
chickens, unwrap, remove the giblets and leave in
the refrigerator for at least 24 hours, to 'mature'.
This will produce a remarkable improvement in
both the taste and texture of your finished dish.

Chicken Tetrazzini

There are two versions of this dish, one made with beans and one with small green broccoli spears. Both are delicious and both are firm favourites with my family. The original version of this recipe included a can of condensed celery soup. I don't advise that now, but should you ever be hard-pressed, the condensed celery soup still offers a quick solution to creamy sauce.

SERVES 4
500g (1 lb) stringless green beans
500g (1 lb) cooked chicken meat, diced
125g (4 oz) mushrooms, roughly chopped or sliced
300ml (½ pint) white sauce (see page 23)
250g (8 oz) flat noodles (tagliatelle)
2 tablespoons grated Parmesan cheese

Boil the beans for 8 minutes, drain and set aside. Add the chicken and mushrooms to the white sauce and heat through. Boil the noodles for 3 minutes, cover and leave to stand in the water for 6 minutes. Drain, mix with the beans in a serving dish and pour the chicken sauce mixture over the top. Sprinkle with the Parmesan to serve.

Chicken with Rosemary

This is a nice easy recipe for a summer evening. Fresh rosemary is best, but dried is fine.

SERVES 4

2 tablespoons flour
4 chicken pieces, skinned
2 tablespoons vegetable oil
300ml (½ pint) chicken stock, approximately (see page 97)
4 tablespoons lemon juice
1 teaspoon chopped fresh rosemary or ½ teaspoon dried
1 teaspoon salt

Flour the chicken portions. Heat the oil in a frying pan and fry the chicken gently for 10 minutes, until golden. Just cover with the stock, then stir in the lemon juice, rosemary and salt. Simmer for 20 minutes, until the sauce thickens. Check the seasoning. Serve with courgettes and shell pasta.

Coronation Chicken

Legend has it that this was the dish developed for the coronation of Queen Elizabeth II, with the intention of being as acceptable as possible to everyone. It wouldn't suit vegetarians or orthodox Jews, but it complies with almost all the dietary requirements of other religions, groups and nationalities. I've modified it slightly here to make it a little more crafty.

It is, without question, one of the most delicious of all buffet party dishes. It is really not very difficult to prepare and is well worth making.

SERVES 4

1 × 1.1 kg (2½ lb) roasting chicken
1 bay leaf
25g (1 oz) butter
1 tablespoon cornflour
4 teaspoons natural yoghurt
4 tablespoons apricot jam
4 tablespoons mayonnaise (not salad cream)
Juice of ½ a lemon
2 tablespoons slivered almonds, toasted
Salt and freshly ground black pepper

Place the chicken and bay leaf in a large pan, season to taste and just cover with water. Cover and gently poach for 45 minutes. Remove from the pan, reserving the liquid, and leave to cool. Skin and bone the chicken and cut into neat pieces.

Melt the butter in a small pan, add the cornflour and blend. Add 150ml (¼ pint) of the reserved chicken stock and bring to the boil, whisking well until smooth. Leave to cool, then whisk in the yoghurt, jam, mayonnaise and lemon juice. Season generously with salt and pepper. Pour the sauce over the chicken pieces, scatter with the almonds and chill for 2 hours.

The Crafty Elastic Chicken

This is my name for a technique of cutting up chickens to provide more dishes than you thought were possible from one bird. It's a technique that's come from a number of different sources, ranging from Fanny Craddock to an American Embassy party (but we won't go into that here, except to remark that like many things from that country American chickens are bigger). Buy yourself one 1.3–1.5kg (3–3½ lb) fairly standard British chicken and stand by.

The method is designed to give you portions that can be casseroled, grilled or fried, and to leave a carcass that can be used to make stock but which will have enough trimmings left on it to make fillings or ingredients for other dishes. The cutting up is described here. It's worth remembering that the first and second times you do it you will find it quite difficult and needing a lot of concentration, but once you become used to it, you will be able to take a chicken apart in this extremely neat and economical way in about two minutes.

The basic tools required are a small 10–15cm (4–6 inch) sharp knife with an easily grasped, firm handle, and a good chopping board on which to work, without any danger of rocking or slipping. Take the chicken out of its wrapping and the plastic bag containing the giblets out of the chicken and follow this step-by-step cutting guide:

- Cut off the leg ends and the wing tips and put to one side.

- Cut off and remove any trussing string that may be on the chicken.

- With the tail pointing towards you, grasp the left leg and pull it gently away from the body. Cut down parallel to the body on the stretched skin. You will find that with a little twist the whole leg will pull right away from the body and lie flat. It will still be attached at the joint.

- Take the knife and, cutting from the neck end of the chicken towards the tail, slice along as close to the body as possible: you'll find the knife runs into the joint and severs it effortlessly. Keep the knife close and parallel to the body and slice until the whole leg and thigh come away.

- Put the leg and thigh with the skin side down and you will see a line of fat at the join between the leg and thigh. Cut down firmly along this line of fat and the leg and thigh will separate cleanly at the joint. Put to one side and repeat the process on the other leg.

- Take each wing and, pulling it slightly out from the body, draw around its base with the knife, cutting in as far as you can, as though you were carving a 2.5cm (1 inch) circle around the joint.

- Twist each wing slightly and you will find that it needs only a small cut with the knife at each socket to remove them completely.

- You now have the carcass with the breasts on it. Running along the side of the chicken on each side is another line of fat just below the meat of the breast. Slice along this on each side, cutting through the small bones and cartilage, until you have cut each breast side loose from the back.

- Lay the large double breast flat, skin side up, and cut across the pointed end 7.5cm (3 inches) from its point to provide one breast portion and divide the remaining breast lengthways into two, using the heel of your hand to press the knife down through the bones.

You should now have three breast pieces, four leg pieces and two wings, making a total of nine portions ready for cooking. In addition to this, you should have the back, the giblets, the wing tips and leg bits to make stock with. Remove the liver from the giblets and collect them in a plastic bag in the freezer until you have enough to make Chicken Liver Pâtés as described on pages 52–53. Rinse the remaining giblets and use to make the chicken stock recipe on page 97.

There follow eight recipes, two pairs of four, one for winter and one for summer, each designed to make four dishes from one chicken. That's where the elastic or stretching bit comes in. You can, of course, use any combination of chicken recipes you like – these just happen to be four that I think make the best and seasonal use of the dissected fowl.

Summer Recipes

Citronelle Soup

Citronelle, or lemon grass, is a new herb to us in Britain, but is fundamental to much cooking in south-east Asia. It's now being used by the fashionable *nouvelle cuisine* restaurants in France to add an intense, but not sharp, lemon flavour and scent to a lot of cooking. You can buy it in supermarkets all over Britain – it looks a bit like a hard-skinned spring onion. It needs a good bashing with a knife handle or a kitchen mallet to release all the flavour. Although it's quite expensive by weight, you need only three stalks to flavour enough soup for four people, so it really isn't a luxury item.

This soup is very pretty and delicate in colour, with a lovely lemon aroma.

SERVES 4
3–4 stalks of lemon grass
1.2 litres (2 pints) chicken stock (see page 97)
1 bunch of spring onions, chopped
50g (2 oz) superfine vermicelli or rice noodles
125g (4 oz) peeled prawns
Salt and freshly ground black pepper

Bruise the lemon grass as described above and add it to the stock. Simmer for 20 minutes. Press the lemon grass to extract all the flavour, then discard. Add the spring onions and vermicelli or rice noodles to the soup and simmer for 5 minutes. Season generously with salt and a little pepper. Add the prawns and heat through. Serve immediately.

Garlic Grilled Chicken Breasts with Cream

This is originally a Turkish recipe. An enterprising restaurateur decided to enrich the classic yoghurt marinade with some rather westernised double cream. The result is an exquisite dish that the sultans would thoroughly have approved of.

SERVES 2

4 tablespoons each double cream and thick natural yoghurt
Juice of ½ a lemon
2 cloves of garlic
1 teaspoon salt
2 chicken breasts (on or off the bone)

Mix the cream, yoghurt and lemon juice together. Crush the garlic with the salt and add to the cream mixture. Score the chicken breasts with a sharp knife diagonally across at 2.5cm (1 inch) intervals. Add to the cream mixture and leave to marinate for at least 2 hours and up to 12 hours, turning occasionally.

Heat the grill to the maximum temperature for at least 10 minutes. Place the chicken breasts in a foil-lined grill pan and grill for 4 minutes each side, until the breasts have crisp brown edges, but are still succulent inside. Serve with rice or hot pitta bread and a salad.

CRAFTY TIP

When grilling meat and poultry, line the grill pan with foil, shiny side up. Not only does this keep your pan clean, it also reflects the heat and speeds up the cooking process.

Stir Fry Chicken with Peppers and Mangetouts

This stir fry recipe is perfect for summer eating – it's quick to prepare, light to eat, and yet has a surprisingly intense flavour. The ingredients are also at their best and cheapest in the summer. Mangetouts are flat peapods where the peas inside have hardly developed. You eat the whole lot, having strung them like runner beans. The flavour is very 'pea' and they're far better value than ordinary peas because there's no waste.

SERVES 4

2 chicken legs
1 large Spanish onion
1 each red and green pepper, cored and seeded
1 clove of garlic
1 cm (1/2 inch) piece fresh root ginger or 1/2 teaspoon ground ginger
1 dessertspoon cornflour
250ml (8 fl oz) water
2 tablespoons soy sauce
2 tablespoons oil
250g (8 oz) mangetouts
Salt and freshly ground black pepper

Remove the meat from the chicken legs and cut into 1cm (1/2 inch) strips across the grain. Cut the onion in half, then cut each half into 1cm (1/2 inch) ribbons. Slice the peppers into similar sized pieces. Crush the garlic and ginger together into a fairly smooth paste. Blend the cornflour, water and soy sauce together.

Heat the oil in a frying pan or wok until it's just below smoking point. Add the garlic and ginger mixture, stir for 30 seconds and, before it browns or burns, add the chicken pieces. Stir those round for about 2 minutes, until opaque all the way through and just starting to brown on the outside. Transfer to a plate. Add the onions, peppers and mangetouts to the pan and stir cook over high heat for 3–4 minutes, until the vegetables are hot right through but still have a crunch. Return the chicken to the pan and mix together with the vegetables. Season with a little salt and pepper, then add the blended cornflour. Stir and toss for 1 minute – the sauce thickens and goes shiny and smooth. Serve hot with rice and, if you like, other Chinese dishes.

Waldorf Salad

This dish was invented, so the story goes, in the old Waldorf Astoria Hotel. It's a very American-style salad – crunchy and munchy rather than limp and lettucy – and has the splendid capacity to be eaten either as a light main course in warm weather, or as a delicious starter. Whatever else it is, it's *not* a side salad and should be eaten on its own. The meat comes from the chicken carcass you've used for stock.

SERVES 4

125g (4 oz) cooked chicken meat, roughly chopped
175g (6 oz) celery, thinly sliced
1 eating apple, quartered then thinly sliced lengthways
1 tablespoon lemon juice
125ml (4 fl oz) mayonnaise (home-made – see page 27 – or proper
  American-style shop bought)
75g (3 oz) walnut pieces
Salt and freshly ground black pepper
Celery leaves to garnish (optional)

Mix together the chicken, celery and apple. Mix the lemon juice into the mayonnaise, then stir into the chicken mixture. Stir in half the walnuts.

Place in lettuce cups, bowls, or one large salad bowl to serve. Garnish with the remaining walnut pieces and, if you like, a few celery leaves.

Winter Recipes

Chicken Barley Soup

A real warming farmhouse-style soup. It's very simple to make and, depending on what vegetables are available, you can vary the ingredients. It's also one of those soups that benefits from being reheated the next day, though it may need a little more liquid, as the barley will absorb the juices.

SERVES 4

50g (2 oz) butter
250g (8 oz) each onion, leek, turnip and carrot, cut into 1cm (¹/₂ inch)
  pieces
125g (4 oz) pearl barley

2 celery sticks, sliced
1 teaspoon salt
Freshly ground black pepper
1.2 litres (2 pints) chicken stock (see page 97)
125g (4 oz) parsley, chopped

Melt the butter in a deep saucepan, add the diced vegetables, pearl barley and celery. Season with the salt and pepper to taste and add the stock. Simmer for 40 minutes, until the vegetables are tender and the barley is swollen and cooked through (test a bit between your teeth to make sure).

To serve, put a spoonful of chopped parsley in each bowl and pour the soup over it, to get a thorough mix and a bright green colour that sets off the more subtle earthy tones of the soup.

Chicken Breasts with Mustard Cream Sauce

This is a chicken adaptation of the great crafty cream sauce but none the worse for that! You can now buy herb flavoured mustards. The particular one I'm thinking of is flavoured with thyme and tarragon, which are perfect herbs for chicken. Ideally, bone the chicken breasts for this dish, cutting off the rib cage and freeing the succulent white meat. Make sure you get the bits of wishbone out as well as they can be wickedly sharp when you're chewing on them unexpectedly. This is quite a grand dish and very rich. It needs a simple starter and I think just potatoes or rice to set it off plus a salad to follow.

SERVES 2
25g (1 oz) each oil and butter
1 clove of garlic, finely chopped
2 chicken breasts
150ml (¼ pint) double cream
1 dessertspoon thyme and tarragon mustard (or any herb mustard)
Salt and freshly ground black pepper
Lemon juice (optional)

Heat together the oil and butter in a frying pan into which the breasts will fit all at once without leaving much space. When the butter is foaming, add the garlic and then the chicken breasts (skin side down). Fry for 3 minutes, turn, lower the heat and fry for another 5 minutes. Season to taste and remove the breasts to a warm place.

Into the pan tip the cream, bring to the boil and stir in the mustard. You may want to check the sauce for balance at this point – a squeeze of lemon juice can sometimes help. Pour the sauce over the chicken immediately or, if you're feeling like a very *nouvelle* presentation, pour the sauce into a shallow oval dish, place the chicken breasts on top and sprinkle delicately with a little very finely chopped tarragon, thyme or even parsley.

Italian Chicken and Peppers

This recipe is an example of how different techniques using the same ingredients produce really different results – compare it with the Chinese Stir Fry Chicken with Peppers and Mangetouts (page 113). Cooked in much larger pieces and much more slowly with different seasonings, the result is a rich, warming casserole which still has a hint of the sun about it to brighten even our coldest winter nights. It is very good with pasta, particularly the broad egg and spinach noodles called tagliatelle – toss the cooked tagliatelle in a little of the casserole's juices and serve as a bed for the casserole.

SERVES 4
2 tablespoons olive oil
2 each chicken thighs, wings and drumsticks
1 red and 2 green peppers, cored, seeded and cut into 2.5cm (1 inch)
    strips
250g (8 oz) onions, cut into 2.5cm (1 inch) strips
1 clove of garlic, chopped
1 teaspoon each dried oregano, basil and thyme
250ml (8 fl oz) pasatta or canned chopped tomatoes mashed with
    1 tablespoon tomato purée
Salt and freshly ground black pepper

Heat the oil in a flameproof casserole and fry the chicken pieces gently until browned all over. Add the peppers, onions and garlic and cook, stirring, for 2 minutes. Season generously and add the herbs and pasatta or mashed tomatoes. Stir to coat all the ingredients thoroughly, then cook in a preheated oven, 180°C (350°F) gas mark 4, for 50 minutes.

You can if you like thicken the sauce with a little blended cornflour, but it's not authentically Italian and shouldn't be necessary if you're eating the dish with pasta, which soaks up the juices.

Chicken Pan-cake

This is quite a spectacular little dish, making a surprising and filling starter. Any odd bits of chicken meat can be used, especially those that you can remove from the carcass after making stock.

SERVES 4

½ teaspoon chili powder
125g (4 oz) Gruyère or Cheddar cheese, grated
125g (4 oz) button mushrooms, sliced
175g (6 oz) cooked chicken meat
300ml (½ pint) white sauce (see page 23)
6 × 25cm (10 inch) pancakes, bought or ready prepared
2 tablespoons fromage frais
25g (1 oz) Parmesan cheese, grated
Salt and freshly ground black pepper

Add the chili powder, half the grated Gruyère or Cheddar cheese, the mushrooms and chicken pieces to the hot white sauce. Heat through thoroughly, stirring, season to taste and set aside.

Place a pancake on a heatproof dish and top with 3 tablespoons of the chicken mixture. Repeat the layers until you have one pancake left (that is, you will finish with chicken mixture on top).

Spread the fromage frais and remaining grated Gruyère or Cheddar cheese over the chicken filling, place the last pancake on top and sprinkle with the Parmesan. Cook the whole 'cake' in a preheated oven, 180°C (350°F) gas mark 4, for 20 minutes or until the whole mixture is thoroughly hot and bubbling and the top has glazed.

Cut into wedges like a cake and serve immediately.

Other Poultry

As well as chicken, there is, of course, a wide range of other birds that we consume with some relish, from the Christmas turkey to the country pigeon. The interest in game, partly because of its health-giving properties (low fat, naturally reared, and so on) and partly because of the rich and intense flavours it provides, has been one of the hallmarks of recent years. It's now very widely available, not only from game dealers and specialist butchers, but also on supermarket shelves.

Turkey Escalopes

It's now possible to obtain very good fillets and escalopes of turkey, which bear a strong resemblance to veal rather than to other poultry. Don't buy the ones that have been adulterated with other meats, water, flavourings or fats – buy the simple meat, cut across the grain in the tradition of veal escalopes. The meat's quite dry, which is an advantage in health terms (it has the lowest saturated fat of any meat available on the general market) but can be a disadvantage in cooking. They work very well with the Mustard Cream Sauce (see page 133) and also make very good turkey Wiener Schnitzels.

I remember these escalopes made with veal from my childhood when an Austrian refugee from the Holocaust lived nearby and had a son my own age. The taste of those delicious morsels lingers yet and the nearest I have ever got to them was made with turkey.

Turkey 'Wiener Schnitzel'

SERVES 4
4 × 175g (6 oz) turkey escalopes or fillets
Juice of 1 lemon
1 egg, beaten
250g (8 oz) fresh white breadcrumbs
2 tablespoons oil
125g (4 oz) unsalted butter

Pound the turkey escalopes between wetted sheets of greaseproof paper, using either a steak mallet or the base of a heavy frying pan or saucepan, until the meat is as thin as you can reasonably get it. Peel off the greaseproof paper and marinate the escalopes in the lemon juice for at least 20 minutes. Then egg and breadcrumb them carefully, pressing the breadcrumbs in firmly. Leave to set. If you have egg and breadcrumbs left over, a double coating doesn't hurt.

Heat the oil and butter together in a large frying pan, which is big enough to take all the escalopes at once if possible. When it's foaming, put in the escalopes and fry for 2 minutes, lower the heat, turn and fry the other side for 4 minutes. Both sides should be golden brown and sealed and because the meat is so thinly beaten inside it will be cooked in this short time. Drain for a moment on crumpled absorbent paper, then serve with noodles or creamed potatoes.

Duck Montmorency

This method of roasting a duck is Chinese-derived and works like a dream. Montmorency was a pre-revolutionary French dukedom in the south-west of France, famous for its cherries and, so legend has it, for a duke who insisted on having them with everything. As it happens, they go particularly well with duck. If you can, use the bitter-sweet cherries known as morellos, as their sharpness counteracts the sweetness of the duck perfectly.

SERVES 4
1 × 1.75 kg (4 lb) oven-ready duck
2 teaspoons arrowroot blended with a little water
425g (15 oz) can morello cherries
Salt and freshly ground black pepper

Place the duck in a colander in the sink and pour over 600ml (1 pint) boiling water. Leave it to dry for 1–2 hours, then roast in a preheated oven, 200°C (400°F) gas mark 6, allowing 20 minutes per 500g (1 lb). Make sure the duck is on a rack over the roasting pan to let the fat come out. When the duck is golden brown, remove from the pan and keep warm.

Place 2 tablespoons of the pan drippings, the blended arrowroot and the cherries and their juice in a pan and bring to the boil until it thickens and clears. Season to taste and serve with the duck, accompanied by creamed potatoes. Have a salad afterwards.

Pheasant with Apples

This is a variation on the Normandy style of cooking, which uses apples, cream and sometimes Calvados. It's particularly delicious with pheasant, a bird we under-rate greatly in this country – except as a target for guns. Even quite a small pheasant will feed three people very generously and a cock, although it's not supposed to have the best flavour, will feed four. The more ancient versions of this recipe suggest you use a whole pheasant, but I prefer to cut it up before cooking it. This recipe uses the traditional rich mixture of double cream and apples. If you worry about the level of cholesterol in your food, or think there's no point in using low-fat game with high-fat cream, substitute crème fraîche, or even natural yoghurt with a dessertspoon of cornflour whisked into it.

You can also make this recipe with chicken.

SERVES 4

1 tablespoon oil
25g (1 oz) butter
1 pheasant, cut into 4 pieces
A fresh bouquet garni of celery, tarragon, thyme and bay leaf
300ml (1/2 pint) fresh (not concentrated) apple juice
150ml (1/4 pint) double cream
2 eating apples, cored and cut into 8–12 sections
Salt and freshly ground black pepper

Heat the oil and butter together in a flameproof casserole and sauté the pheasant pieces for about 5 minutes, until well browned. Add the bouquet garni and plenty of seasoning, then pour over the apple juice. Cook in a preheated oven, 180°C (350°F) gas mark 4, for 45–50 minutes, until the pheasant is cooked through. Transfer to a serving dish.

Pour the sauce into a pan, add the cream and bring to the boil. Melt a little more butter in a separate frying pan and fry the apple pieces very lightly until they are just heated through and coloured. Arrange around the edge of the dish. Pour the sauce over the pheasant.

If you like the sauce very thick, reduce it by boiling, but leaving it quite liquid allows people to mop it up with plenty of French bread – it's so deliciously flavoured.

Serve with mashed potatoes or little triangles of toast or fried bread – the traditional way in the Normandy valleys it comes from.

Pigeon Casserole

This is one of the cheapest and nicest ways of getting the flavour of game, without the trouble of hanging and the other paraphernalia that often goes with cooking fur and feathers.

SERVES 4

1 tablespoon vegetable oil
25g (1 oz) butter
4 pigeons
250g (8 oz) button onions
A fresh bouquet garni of celery, tarragon, thyme and bay leaf
300ml (1/2 pint) chicken stock, approximately (see page 97)
250g (8 oz) button mushrooms
Grated rind and juice of 1 orange
Salt and freshly ground black pepper

Heat the oil and butter together in a pan and sauté the pigeons for 5 minutes, turning, until browned all over. Place in a casserole. Brown the onions lightly in the pan, then add to the pigeons with the bouquet garni. Pour over enough stock to cover and season well. Cook in a preheated oven, 180°C (350°F) gas mark 4, for 1 hour.

Add the mushrooms and the orange rind and juice and cook for 30 minutes. Remove the bouquet garni, season to taste and serve with lots of mashed potato. The gravy can be thickened, but it's nice as it is.

Rabbit Casserole

This is also known, I suspect, as rabbit stew and, with a bit of pastry on the top, as rabbit pie in various parts of Britain. It's an old country recipe using ingredients normally ready to hand. A wild rabbit and organically grown vegetables can turn this modest dish into a feast.

SERVES 4

2 tablespoons flour
1 teaspoon dried mixed herbs
1 rabbit, jointed
2 tablespoons oil
25g (1 oz) butter
1 onion, sliced
500g (1 lb) carrots, cut into 2.5cm (1 inch) chunks
300ml (½ pint) chicken stock or water

Mix the flour and herbs together and use to coat the rabbit pieces. Heat the oil and butter together in a frying pan and fry the rabbit until golden brown on all sides. Pile into a casserole into which the pieces just fit – an oval one is the traditional shape. Add the onion and carrots to the frying pan and stir round until they're thoroughly coated with the butter and oil. Add to the casserole, pour in the stock or water and cover tightly. Cook in a preheated oven, 150°C (300°F) gas mark 2, for 1½ hours, until the rabbit is completely tender.

Jugged Hare

This is the old English way of cooking rabbit's rather grander cousin – the hare. A hare is supposed to feed six people, but I've never found one tender enough to cook that would feed more than four good appetites cooked this way – it's so delicious. Traditionally, the cooking dish was a large earthenware jug because, narrow at the top and spacious at the bottom, it allowed the least evaporation. You can use the modern Cataplana casserole (available in most cookshops these days), or one of the tall ceramic pots (sometimes used for cooking beans or storing bread) standing in a dish with at least 2.5cm (1 inch) depth of water (known as a *bain-marie*). The important thing is slow gentle cooking with as little evaporation as possible. Foil on the top helps as well.

SERVES 4
1 large hare, jointed
4 tablespoons seasoned flour
2 tablespoons oil
50g (2 oz) butter
2 large onions, chopped
450ml (¾ pint) beef stock (water would do)
250g (8 oz) button onions
500g (1 lb) button mushrooms
4 tablespoons redcurrant jelly

Roll the hare joints in the seasoned flour. Heat the oil and half the butter in a large pan and fry the hare pieces until well browned. Place in a tall narrow topped casserole or jug. Fry the chopped onions in the same fat, then add to the casserole with the stock. Cover, place in a *bain-marie* (see above) and cook in a preheated oven, 150°C (300°F) gas mark 2, for 2 hours.

Melt the remaining butter and fry the button onions and mushrooms lightly. Add to the casserole with the redcurrant jelly. If the sauce is too thin, mix a little of the remaining seasoned flour with 1–2 tablespoons water and stir that it in as well. Cook for 20 minutes, until the sauce has thickened and the onions and mushrooms are cooked.

Serve with lots and lots of mashed potato and red cabbage.

Venison Pasty

This is a crafty adaptation of a Scottish recipe. Unlike the Cornish version of the pasty, it is not wrapped in pastry but has a pastry lid placed on top of it. It's a marvellous way of using stewing venison – quite cheap nowadays.

SERVES 4

1–2 tablespoons oil
1 kg (2 lb) boneless stewing venison, cut into 2.5 cm (1 inch) cubes
50g (2 oz) butter
500g (1 lb) each onions and turnips, cut into 1 cm (½ inch) pieces
250g (8 oz) each carrots and parsnips, cut into 1 cm (½ inch) pieces
2 bay leaves
Pinch of dried thyme
2 tablespoons flour
1 tablespoon tomato purée
1 teaspoon Dijon mustard
1 quantity Shortcrust Pastry (see page 201)
1 egg, beaten
Salt and freshly ground black pepper

Heat the oil in a heavy-based frying pan and fry the venison until browned. Remove from the pan and set aside. Melt the butter in the pan and add the vegetables, bay leaves and thyme. Simmer over a very low heat for about 10 minutes, until the vegetables are soft but still have a little texture left. Sprinkle over the flour and stir. Add the venison and enough water to come halfway up the side of the pan. Add the tomato purée and mustard, bring to the boil, then cover and simmer on a very low heat until the meat is tender; depending on the cut of venison, this may take anything from 45 minutes to 1½ hours. You may need to add more water as it cooks, but the final sauce should be thick and rich. Pour into a pie dish almost to the brim and season.

 Cut off a quarter of the pastry and roll it into a sausage shape long enough to go round the dish. Dampen the rim of the dish and position the pastry sausage. Roll the rest of the pastry out into a smooth sheet large enough to cover the dish. Dampen the pastry sausage, lay the sheet of pastry over the dish and press the edge down with your thumb and forefinger, making a pinched effect all the way round. Trim off any excess, cut a slit in the top and fix the traditional leaves made from the pastry trimmings. Brush with beaten egg and bake in a preheated oven, 220°C (425°F) gas mark 7, for 25 minutes, until the pastry is golden brown and the whole pie bubbling hot.

 Serve with mashed potatoes and, if you want to be authentic, curly kale.

Meat

Over the last few years the pattern of meat consumption has changed quite considerably in this country. About five or six years ago I remember reading one of those 'do you have the right lifestyle to live till you're 200' type quizzes in a Sunday supplement. One of the questions was, 'Have you eaten, or do you eat, more than 8 oz of meat every three days?' My instinctive answer was, 'Of course I do', but when I actually added it up and worked it out over the previous fortnight, it turned out that it wasn't true. I think most of us have gradually cut the amount of red meat we eat – that's certainly the evidence of both government and food industry research. But unless you are a dedicated vegetarian, or one of the new demi-veg devotees, I think it's a pity to lose entirely the great pleasures of meat. Perhaps we should follow the example set in the Far East and other parts of the world where meat is a luxury and is used as a savoury – something to give the rest of the meal spike and focus, rather than a main ingredient in its own right.

I must admit to having a very personal approach to meat. That doesn't mean I don't like it, it merely means I tend to have great surging enthusiasms for certain things, but a quite 'take it or leave it' attitude towards many people's favourite sorts of meat dishes. For me, you can forget hot roast beef, for example, on condition that I have a plateful of the vegetables, roast potatoes and parsnips, carrots, plenty of Yorkshire pudding and some of the gravy. I can manage, and often do, very well without the beef itself. But when it's cold and it's cut in thick, pink slices to be eaten with hot baked potatoes, some home-made chutney or possibly a pickle or two, my tastebuds are tantalised. The reverse is true for lamb. Eaten roasted, hot and crisp with the fat succulent and the meat firm and sweet, it's one of my great passions, but cold roast lamb is just another form of sustenance. I apologise for these eccentricities, but I hope you'll find in my list of true enthusiasms a wide range of meat dishes that you will enjoy.

Most of these recipes are extremely simple but many of them are rich. At the heart of these is, perhaps, the ultimate 'crafty cooking' recipe: Steak with Mustard Cream Sauce. It has a number of adaptations and developments but for ease, oohs and aahs it has no equal. Of all recipes, it is the craftiest and I commend it to you and your family and friends.

Roast Beef

I'm beginning the beef section with roast beef because, of all the dishes known to British cooks, this is the one about which people tend to have strong feelings. I've a few tips about roast beef, the central one of which is that I prefer it cold, as I think you then get the full delicate flavour of the beef. But whether you eat it hot or cold, do choose the right joint. The modern habit of buying very lean joints like topside is a mistake for roasting as these are better suited to braising. For roasting you need a joint with a little bit of fat marbled through it and, certainly, covering it. Sirloin, which is the most expensive, is ideal, but so too is the butchers' favourite, fore rib. Very few people know about it and I am indebted to Josceline Dimbleby for introducing me to it. Without any question, it is the best value (about half the price of sirloin), it has the best flavour and is a marvellous joint to roast. You can have it boned and rolled or on the bone. If you have it on the bone, though, ask the butcher to chine it to loosen the flat side of the rib, which makes it easier to carve.

It is much more economic to buy a large piece of beef to roast because the meat shrinks much less in relation to its original weight and you don't lose so much in the cooking. You can always use it for other dishes afterwards, even if you don't share my preference for cold roast beef. For example, if you slice the cold meat thinly and smother it in a vinaigrette or lemonette dressing which has a good handful of parsley and chives mixed in it and leave it to marinate for a couple of hours, you'll have Beef Parisienne – a great French favourite served both as a first course in small quantities and as a main meal.

If you want to cook smaller pieces of beef, do please braise or pot roast them. Again, it's more economic and the flavour will be better in the end, too. You can also use leaner cuts of beef, if that's your inclination. The following recipe allows for a largish joint of beef for roasting to be eaten hot and/or cold, and to have use made of the leftover joint afterwards.

1 large roasting joint – wing rib, fore rib or sirloin
Salt and freshly ground black pepper

To begin with, weigh the joint or have it weighed. If it has its bone left in, allow a cooking time of 17 minutes per 500g (1 lb). Without the bone, allow 20 minutes per 500g (1 lb). Preheat the oven to extremely hot, 230°C (450°F) gas mark 8. Don't worry, it won't be at this temperature all the time – it's merely to seal the meat before allowing it to cook at a lower temperature. Season the joint generously and put it, fat side up, in a roasting pan and place it in the oven. Immediately, lower the heat to 180°C (350°F) gas mark 4. Leave the meat to cook for whatever time you calculated. Remove from the oven and rest it for another 5 minutes per 500g (1 lb) before beginning to carve. It won't get cold but will cook right on, gently absorbing its own juices and becoming very tender to carve.

If you're eating it hot, serve with its own juices made from the pan liquid and its carving juice, mustard and horseradish sauce, roast potatoes and all the usual trimmings. If you're serving it cold, let it cool without putting it into the fridge until it's really cold on the outside. That way it will stay much more succulent to carve. It will be pink in the middle but cooked right through. If you like your beef much better done, may I once again suggest braising as it will keep much more succulent while cooking all the way through.

Braised Beef

Braising is basically a method of roasting with moisture involved. The meat, often quite a lean and dry piece, whether lamb or beef, can be placed on a bed of vegetables and flavourings and cooked in a sealed container. The method is also known as pot roasting and though I'm not going to give a detailed set of recipes, I will describe the method and suggest various flavours. Make sure the meat is trimmed and, if possible, boned and that it fits as closely as possible in size inside the casserole.

You need a layer of vegetables and/or liquid, not more than 2.5cm (1 inch) deep, underneath the meat and it should not at all be completely covered by liquid because it is meant to cook in steam and heat, rather than be immersed in liquid or fat.

Brown the meat first before you put it into the casserole and on to the vegetables and use plenty of flavouring and seasonings as these will penetrate the meat from underneath.

Don't use too fierce a heat in the oven: it should be between 170–180°C (325–350°F) gas marks 3 and 4. The meat will need to cook for about 20–25 minutes per 500g (1 lb) and will probably turn brown right through as it's difficult to braise rare.

Ideal cuts for beef are topside, silverside or H-bone and, for lamb or mutton, rolled shoulder or the top half of a leg.

Some flavourings:

For lamb try celery and leeks (about 250g [8 oz] of each) with some marjoram and thyme.

For beef try carrots, onions and garlic with cider (not malt) vinegar – about 4 tablespoons – to flavour it, plus a bay leaf and some parsley.

For brisket, 4 tablespoons of soy sauce with 500g (1 lb) of chopped onions, a couple of cloves of garlic and 2 pieces of star anise – a Chinese spice that produces a marvellous exotic flavour.

In all cases, don't forget to brown the meat first, to season it generously and to add not more than half a cup of water to the vegetable mixture before you put it in the oven. You carve in the normal way and you can either serve the vegetables as a kind of bed for the meat, or purée them into a rich thick flavoursome sauce to go with the meat and other fresh vegetables you've cooked on the side.

CRAFTY TIP

Tougher beef makes the most wonderful casseroles, succulent and rich. Use beef that's not too tender to start with so that when you cook it you get the delicious flavours that slow cooking and the dissolving of the tendon and muscular structure of the beef produces – rich luscious sauces and tender chunks of meat.

Carbonnade of Beef

Every country cooks its beef in whatever wine or beer it has locally. This recipe from Belgium uses lager to make a lovely rich gravy.

SERVES 6
1kg (2 lb) stewing beef
50g (2 oz) flour
1 tablespoon vegetable oil
25g (1 oz) butter
500g (1 lb) onions, sliced
300ml (½ pint) lager
300ml (½ pint) beef stock
Bouquet garni (bought ready prepared)
Salt and freshly ground black pepper
2 tablespoons chopped parsley to garnish

Cut the meat into pieces roughly half the size of a postcard and 5mm (¼ inch) thick. Dust with some of the flour. Heat the oil and butter together in a frying pan and fry the meat for about 5 minutes, until brown. Transfer to a casserole. Fry the onions in the same oil for 2 minutes. Sprinkle with the remaining flour, then mix with the beef. Rinse out the hot frying pan with the lager and add to the beef with the stock. Season to taste, add the bouquet garni and cook in a preheated oven, 170°C (325°F) gas mark 3, for 3 hours. Remove the bouquet garni. Sprinkle with the parsley and serve with mashed potatoes. Follow with any vegetables served as a course on their own.

Hungarian Goulash

Three things always seem to be associated with Hungary – gipsies, violins and goulash. I don't think any of them are unique to Hungary but they do all seem to have reached their high point in that country. This recipe is not for those who like their food plain, simple and 'not messed about'. It's one of the richest and most delicious stews ever invented. The gipsies and violins are up to you!

SERVES 6

1 tablespoon vegetable oil
25g (1 oz) butter
1 kg (2 lb) chuck steak, cut into 2.5cm (1 inch) cubes
1 large Spanish onion, chopped
2 cloves of garlic, crushed
900ml (1½ pints) beef or chicken stock (cubes will do)
150g (5 oz) can tomato purée
2 tablespoons paprika
1 tablespoon cornflour blended with 1 tablespoon water
Salt and freshly ground black pepper
150ml (¼ pint) soured cream to serve

Heat the oil and butter in a large flameproof casserole and fry the meat until lightly browned. Add the onion and garlic and stir until well coated in the fat. Add the stock, tomato purée and paprika and season well. Stir thoroughly to ensure the tomato paste and paprika are evenly distributed. Cover and simmer on top of the stove or in a preheated oven, 180°C (350°F) gas mark 4, for 2 hours. Add the blended cornflour and simmer until thickened.

Spoon into serving bowls and top with a good spoonful of soured cream at the last minute. Serve with noodles.

You can add mushrooms or potatoes to the goulash if you wish to make it go further – the Hungarians aren't purists in the matter, and neither am I!

Daube Macaroniade

One of the secrets of crafty cooking is not to give yourself too much to do. This dish from Provence can be cooked in advance and just heated up on the day you want to eat it. The macaroni shells are traditional in this part of France, which is so close to the Italian border.

SERVES 6

1 kg (2 lb) shin of beef
1 tablespoon vegetable oil
2 onions, chopped
400g (14 oz) can tomatoes
600ml (1 pint) beef stock
1 teaspoon garlic salt
2 bay leaves
1 teaspoon dried thyme
50g (2 oz) black olives, stoned (optional)

Cut the meat into 2.5cm (1 inch) cubes; do not throw away the fat and sinew. Heat the oil in a flameproof casserole and fry the meat for about 5 minutes, until browned. Add the onions and fry for 5 minutes, then add the tomatoes and stock. Season with the garlic salt, add the bay leaves and thyme and simmer for 2 hours; the sauce will gradually thicken.

Five minutes before serving, remove the bay leaves and add the olives, if liked. Serve with macaroni shells or pieces cooked in the usual way (follow packet directions), using some of the sauce from the meat to mix in and moisten them before serving. A green salad is nice with this.

Steak, Shellfish and Mushroom Pie

Until the nineteenth century an English casserole almost always had a pie crust, so I've put one on this. It can be made without, of course. This dish needs a little advance planning. For a special occasion, it's normally greeted with all the 'oohs and ahhs' you could wish. In its original form it was made with oysters – when they cost a pound a barrel. If you're feeling rich you can still use them, but mussels make a more than acceptable substitute.

SERVES 4

25g (1 oz) butter
500g (1 lb) stewing steak, cubed
1 tablespoon flour
1 onion, chopped
125g (4 oz) button mushrooms, halved
600ml (1 pint) beef stock
125g (4 oz) mussels, cleaned (see page 92)
240g (7½ oz) packet frozen puff pastry, thawed
Beaten egg or milk to glaze

Melt the butter in a pan and fry the meat for 5 minutes, until browned. Sprinkle with the flour and brown again. Add the onion and mushrooms, cover with the stock and simmer for about 2–2½ hours, or until tender.

Cook the mussels in boiling salted water for 5 minutes; discard any that do not open. Remove them from the shells and add to the steak. Transfer the mixture to a 1.2 litre (2 pint) pie dish.

Roll out the pastry and use to cover the dish. Flute the edges and cut a cross in the centre. Brush with beaten egg or milk. Bake in a preheated oven, 200°C (400°F) gas mark 6, for 30–35 minutes. Serve with boiled potatoes and hot buttered beetroot.

Steak

Though I've had some wonderful steaks in my time in many parts of the world, plain grilled steak is not one of my favourite dishes. It takes a bit of skill to get right, but I prefer meat with a few flavourings and additions. Here are four ways with steak, beginning with that ultimate crafty cooking dish, as promised.

Steak with Mustard Cream Sauce

The ultimate crafty cooking dish! The trick with this is to make enough sauce as people always scrape it off the plate with anything available – spoons, bread, fingers or even, in the privacy of one's home, the tongue – so good is it. The steak itself almost fades into the background. The same sauce has been used successfully with *magrets* of duck (duck breast steaks with their skin removed), turkey escalopes, chicken breasts and pieces of monkfish. It's pretty good on lobster tails, too, if you can get them. But there is no question that it began with steak.

SERVES 4
1 tablespoon olive or peanut oil
4 × 250g (8 oz) sirloin steaks at least 1 cm (¾ inch) thick, trimmed
300ml (½ pint) double cream
1 heaped tablespoon French grain mustard
Salt and freshly ground black pepper

Heat a heavy-based frying pan into which the steaks will all fit at once until it's very hot. Add the oil and swirl round, then add the steaks. Allow them to seal on one side for 45 seconds–1 minute, turn them over and let them seal again, keeping the heat up really high. If you like your steak rare allow another 2 minutes on the second side, 3 minutes for medium rare, and 4 for ruined. Transfer the steaks to a serving dish and season to taste.

Taking your courage in your hands, pour all the cream at once into the hot pan. Add the mustard and stir it in thoroughly, then bring the cream to the boil. Do not worry, it will not separate. Allow it to thicken and mix well with the mustard. Pour over the steak and serve immediately.

Nothing very much is needed to go with this dish except something to mop up the sauce. Mashed potatoes and plenty of French bread prevent the table deteriorating into vulgarity. A crisp green salad afterwards is the perfect foil.

Steak Diane

This is essentially a restaurant dish — one of those that is cooked at your table with a certain amount of flamboyance and 'flambéance'. It's none the worse for that, although the flambéing is an optional extra.

SERVES 4
1 tablespoon oil
25g (1 oz) butter
4 fillet steaks 2.5cm (1 inch) thick
1 onion, chopped
250g (8 oz) mushrooms, sliced
1 tablespoon Worcestershire sauce
8 anchovy fillets (optional)

Heat a heavy-based frying pan into which all the steaks will fit at once. Add the oil and butter and when hot add the steaks and seal for 30 seconds per side. Stir in the onion and mushrooms and cook for 4 minutes, turning the steaks once during this time. Pour the Worcestershire sauce over the steaks and allow to sizzle. Serve at once, piling the oniony–mushroomy gravy on to each one. Decorate with a criss-cross pattern of anchovy fillets for extra savouriness if you wish.

They are nicest served with a baked potato dish and a green vegetable.

Steak au Poivre

To be made properly this dish needs peppercorns that have been crushed, rather than ground — you want chunks of pepper rather than finely ground bits. A mixture of white and black is traditional for this kind of cooking.

SERVES 4
4 × 175g (6 oz) porterhouse or entrecôte steaks
2 tablespoons crushed peppercorns
1 tablespoon cooking oil
25g (1 oz) butter
1 tablespoon brandy, warmed (optional)

Trim the steaks so that they look neat and rub the pepper into both sides, pressing the chunks into the steak. Leave for at least 20 minutes and up to 2 hours for the flavours to penetrate.

Heat the oil and butter together in a heavy-based pan into which all the steaks will fit at once and cook them for 1½ minutes on one side. Turn – don't worry if bits of the pepper fall off – and cook for 2 minutes for rare, 3 minutes for medium rare. Transfer to a serving plate and pour over the juices. If you wish, leave the juices in the pan, pour in the brandy and ignite it carefully, making sure there's nothing close by that can be singed. Wait until the flames die down, then pour over the steaks and serve.

CRAFTY TIP

To crush peppercorns, put them in a heavy-duty plastic bag, cover it with a couple of thicknesses of tea towel, then bash either with a rolling pin or the base of a heavy frying pan.

Steak with Stilton

Classic English ingredients these, Stilton cheese and good beef, with a little touch of the Raj added to make it an outstanding dish.

SERVES 4

175g (6 oz) Stilton cheese, rind removed
25g (1 oz) butter
2 tablespoons mango chutney
4 × 175g (6 oz) entrecôte steaks
Salt and freshly ground black pepper

Mash the Stilton with the butter and chutney until smooth. Lightly season the steaks and cook under a preheated hot grill for 1 minute. Turn over and grill for 5 minutes. Turn the steaks again and spread with the cheese mixture. Grill for 1½–2 minutes, until the cheese is bubbling and golden and thoroughly melted. Serve immediately with sauté potatoes, chips or Pommes de Terre Dauphinoise (see page 173).

Mince

One thing I've learned over the years is the great advantages and virtues of mince. We tend to look down on it in this country as a kind of second best food, though we certainly consume enough of it in the form of hamburgers from various fast-food outlets! But, in fact, it's a wonderful and versatile way of using meat, and it's also very economical.

Cabbage Rolls

Versions of this dish exist from Poland to the Red Sea. I suspect they all have a connection at some stage with Jewish cooking. Some are sweet and sour, some use rice instead of breadcrumbs, others use various meats.

SERVES 4
500g (1 lb) minced lamb or beef
40g (1½ oz) fresh breadcrumbs
1 egg
4 tablespoons tomato sauce
2 tablespoons Worcestershire sauce
16 large cabbage leaves
350ml (12 fl oz) can tomato juice
1 tablespoon each lemon juice and brown sugar
1 teaspoon Mediterranean herbs
Salt and freshly ground black pepper

Mix together the meat, breadcrumbs, egg, tomato and Worcestershire sauces and salt and pepper to taste. Boil the cabbage leaves for 1 minute, then drain. Put a heaped tablespoon of the meat mixture onto each leaf, roll up like a

CRAFTY TIP

Use a couple of the large coarse outer cabbage leaves – ones you wouldn't use for the rolls – to line the pan. That way, if anything sticks to the bottom of the dish it's the old unusable leaves rather than the parcels themselves, which then lift out very easily.

package and place in a baking dish in neat rows. Mix the tomato juice, lemon juice, sugar and herbs together and season highly. Pour over the cabbage rolls and bake in a preheated oven, 180°C (350°F) gas mark 4, for 50 minutes. Serve with mashed potatoes.

Meat Balls with Ginger Gravy

This is an adaptation of a German dish called *Sauerbraten*. The Germans make it with the sort of beef we'd roast, but this version is cheaper and delicious, capturing some of the very unusual flavours of the original dish. However much you may be surprised at the ingredients, stick with them – you will be delighted with the result.

SERVES 4

750g (1½ lb) minced beef
2 tablespoons malt vinegar
2 tablespoons tomato sauce
1 egg, beaten
1 teaspoon garlic salt
½ teaspoon each dried parsley and thyme
1 tablespoon beef dripping or oil
300ml (½ pint) beef stock (approximately)
50g (2 oz) ginger biscuits, finely crushed
1 tablespoon German or mild English mustard
Salt and freshly ground black pepper

Mix the meat, vinegar, tomato sauce, egg, garlic salt, herbs and seasoning together. Knead until smooth, then shape into balls about 3.5cm (1½ inches) diameter.

Melt the dripping or oil in a frying pan wide enough to take all the meat balls in one layer. Fry for about 5 minutes, until lightly browned. Pour in enough stock almost to cover them and simmer gently for 25 minutes.

Transfer the meat balls to a warmed serving dish. Add the crushed biscuits to the liquid in the pan, stirring steadily until you have a smooth purée. Add the mustard and bring to the boil, when it will thicken and darken. If the sauce tastes too sweet, add another 1–2 teaspoons vinegar and bring to the boil again.

Pour over the meat balls and serve with mashed potatoes, and red cabbage cooked slowly with a little sliced onion and grated apple. It may sound bizarre but it tastes marvellous!

Cauliflower Lasagne

A fabulous crafty and economical variation of one of the classic Italian pasta dishes. If you think it reminds you of one of Britain's favourites, cauliflower cheese, you're quite right. The Anglo-Italian combination is almost irresistible. Trust me with the technique for the lasagne – it is really crafty and efficient.

SERVES 4

2 tablespoons vegetable oil
500g (1 lb) minced beef
1 onion, chopped
1 clove of garlic, crushed
400g (14 oz) can tomatoes
2 teaspoons dried basil
3 tablespoons flour
900ml (1½ pints) milk
50g (2 oz) butter
175g (6 oz) cheese, grated
1 small cauliflower, broken into small florets
250g (8 oz) lasagne, soaked for 5 minutes in hot water
Salt and freshly ground black pepper

Heat the oil in a pan and fry the meat, onion and garlic for 5 minutes. Season to taste. Add the tomatoes and basil and simmer for 10 minutes.

Meanwhile, make a white sauce: mix the flour with a little of the milk, add the butter and the rest of the milk, then bring to the boil and whisk gently until it thickens. Add half the cheese and season to taste.

Butter a baking dish and arrange the cauliflower in an even layer over the bottom, seasoning well. Cover with a third of the cheese sauce, then a layer of lasagne, then half the meat mixture, then a little more cheese sauce. Repeat the layers, finishing with a layer of lasagne covered with cheese sauce. Sprinkle with the remaining cheese and dot butter over the top if you like. Cook in a preheated oven, 180°C (350°F) gas mark 4, for 45–50 minutes. A green salad is nice with this.

American Meat Loaf

In America meat loaf is *the* weekend dish. It's always made with beef and is always very easy to make. It has a wide range of variations depending upon the ethnic background of the American family making it: Germans might use caraway seeds, Poles might add some chopped sausage. This version is essentially an Italian American meat loaf. Don't try serving it with Italian additions, by the way. The right thing to eat with it is mashed potatoes, corn on the cob and plenty of gravy made from the pan drippings.

SERVES 4
500g (1 lb) minced beef
2 slices white bread, soaked in milk
1 onion, chopped and lightly fried
1 teaspoon each garlic salt, dried oregano and chopped parsley
1 tablespoon grated Parmesan cheese
1 egg, beaten

OPTIONAL EXTRAS:
4 slices Cheddar cheese
6 tablespoons tomato ketchup
125g (4 oz) mushrooms, chopped

Put all the ingredients in a large bowl and squelch it all together – the mixture should be fairly dry and firm. Shape it into a loaf, place on a baking sheet and cook in a preheated oven, 190°C (375°F) gas mark 5, for 35 minutes, or 40 if you like it well done.
Optional extras: Drape it with slices of cheese, or pour a layer of tomato ketchup right along the middle, or press chopped mushrooms onto the top . . . or all three! . . . before cooking.

CRAFTY TIP

Casseroles and most made dishes like moussaka reheat wonderfully. Many people think the flavours blend so much better overnight that they make them a day in advance. The spicier the dish the more this works. This is not the same, though, as making and then freezing them.

Moussaka

This dish comes from the eastern Mediterranean and is variously claimed by the Turks and the Greeks. Just to be eccentric, this is a Yugoslav version, nonetheless authentic, because when it was first developed the present borders hardly existed. The real difference with this version (not unique to Yugoslavia) is that it uses potatoes as well as aubergines. A much more economic way of eating but also, to my mind, better to the tooth as well, as it gives a little more chew to what can otherwise be a dish that has very little firm texture. Once again, lamb is the traditional meat but beef works equally well.

SERVES 4

500g (1 lb) minced lamb or beef, preferably lamb
1 onion, chopped
1 clove of garlic, chopped
400g (14 oz) can tomatoes
1/2 teaspoon each oregano and thyme
250g (8 oz) potatoes, sliced
500g (1 lb) aubergines, sliced
150g (5 oz) carton natural yoghurt
1 egg
Salt and freshly ground black pepper

Fry the meat, onion and garlic, with no extra fat, until brown. Add the tomatoes, herbs, and salt and pepper to taste and cook gently for 10 minutes.

Arrange the potatoes in a buttered dish, cover with half the meat mixture then a layer of aubergines. Cover with the rest of the meat and top with the remainder of the aubergines. Cook in a preheated oven, 180°C (350°F) gas mark 4, for 20 minutes.

Mix the yoghurt and egg together and pour *gently* over the aubergines. Cook for another 10 minutes. Serve with rice.

Bobotie

This comes from the Cape Malay cooks, who were once brought to South Africa to cook for the British and Afrikaner burghers and farmers. They spice their food with flavourings from their own countries and this particular dish, which began very much as a servant meal made from the leftovers of the top table, has become a firm favourite not only with South Africans but with anyone who's ever had the pleasure of tasting it. You can use beef but, more traditionally, lamb is used. One or two of the additions may seem a little surprising – stick with it, it's worth it in the end! It's normally eaten in Cape Malay families, by the way, with rice that's been cooked with a pinch of turmeric and a small handful of raisins or sultanas.

SERVES 4

2 eggs
150ml (¼ pint) milk
500g (1 lb) minced lamb
2 slices white bread, crusts removed, soaked in milk
1 onion, chopped
1 teaspoon each garlic salt, curry powder and turmeric
50g (2 oz) apricot jam
50g (2 oz) slivered almonds

Set aside one egg, the milk and the almonds. Mix all the other ingredients (including the apricot jam!) together until blended, then place in a 3.5–5cm (1½–2 inch) deep casserole dish. Sprinkle with the almonds and bake in a preheated oven, 180°C (350°F) gas mark 4, for 45 minutes.

Beat the remaining egg and milk together to make a custard, pour it over the mixture and bake for another 20 minutes, until the custard has set and blended all the savoury juices together.

The Real Bolognese Sauce

The food of Bologna is famous all over Italy for its richness and, made properly, this sauce is a far cry from the runny mess we have come to expect with our spaghetti. By the way, although spaghetti is traditional, I prefer tagliatelle – the ribbon noodles cooked as on page 78.

4 tablespoons olive oil
250g (8 oz) lean minced beef
250g (8 oz) onion, finely chopped
1 clove of garlic, chopped
50g (2 oz) chicken livers, chopped
50g (2 oz) carrot, grated
400g (14 oz) can tomatoes
2 tablespoons tomato purée
Salt and freshly ground black pepper
1 teaspoon each dried basil and oregano
1/2 teaspoon dried thyme

Heat the oil in a pan and sauté the beef until brown. Add the onion, garlic, chicken livers and carrot and sauté for 1 minute more before stirring in the tomatoes and tomato purée. Then season to taste and simmer for 45 minutes, adding a little water when necessary to keep the sauce moist. Add the herbs 5 minutes before serving.

Lamb

Mint Glazed Lamb Chops

SERVES 4
4–8 loin or chump chops
1 tablespoon vegetable oil
1 tablespoon garlic salt
4 tablespoons mint jelly

Preheat the grill for 10 minutes at maximum. Brush the chops with the oil and grill for 4 minutes. Turn them over, season with the garlic salt, then spread with the mint jelly. Grill for another 5 minutes. Before serving, spoon the drippings back over the meat – delicious!

Make your own mint jelly by adding a couple of handfuls of fresh mint to apple jelly when you're making it in the autumn. It's a wonderful storecupboard standby, delicious with all kinds of lamb.

Milanese Lamb Cutlets

A crisp lemony coating and tender moist meat make this an unusual way of eating lamb chops. A dish to cook when you're in a hurry but still want to impress.

SERVES 4

8 best end of neck cutlets, chined (this is with only the long bone left on them)
1 egg, beaten
75g (3 oz) breadcrumbs (a packet is fine), mixed with 2 tablespoons grated lemon rind
150ml (¼ pint) vegetable oil
25g (1 oz) butter

Dip the cutlets in the beaten egg, then the breadcrumb mixture. Heat the oil and butter together and fry the cutlets for about 8 minutes on each side, until golden. Serve with sauté potatoes or chips, and courgettes sliced and cooked in a little butter in a covered pan for 2 minutes.

Nico's Lamb with Garlic Sauce

This exquisite and very grand dish is extremely easy to make and a superb centrepiece for any dinner party. I first ate it at the restaurant of one of the greatest self-taught chefs in the world – Nico Ladenis, who's run a series of multi-starred restaurants for years. Although there's plenty of garlic in the sauce, the way it's made makes it a subtle suggestion rather than a blow between the eyes.

SERVES 4

*1 best end of neck of lamb (rack), chined and prepared for roasting (ask
    your butcher to do this for you)*
1 egg, beaten
20g (³/4 oz) fresh breadcrumbs
2 tablespoons chopped parsley
1 teaspoon rosemary, crushed

FOR THE SAUCE:

1 potato, cubed
4 cloves of garlic
300ml (¹/2 pint) milk, or milk and single cream mixed
Salt and freshly ground black pepper

Make sure there are 8 chops in the rack (2 for each person). Peel away the skin from the fat side of the rack and brush with beaten egg. Mix together the breadcrumbs and herbs and press onto the fat to form a thick coating. Place, fat side upwards, in an ovenproof dish into which it will fit comfortably. Roast at the top of a preheated oven, 200°C (400°F) gas mark 6, for 20 minutes for pink and 25 minutes for fully done lamb.

Meanwhile, boil the potato and garlic in the milk for about 15 minutes, until soft. Season generously and purée in a food processor or blender, or push through a sieve until the mixture is absolutely smooth.

To serve, cut the rack of lamb into individual chops and use the sauce either as a bed in the *nouvelle cuisine* style, or dribble some over the lamb and serve the rest in a sauceboat. New potatoes and green beans or broccoli are superb with this.

CRAFTY TIP

To mix breadcrumbs with another ingredient, for example, grated orange or lemon rind, chopped herbs, paprika, place in a paper bag and shake well. If the mixture is to be used as a coating, place the meat in the bag and shake until evenly covered. It works just as well for flour and spices.

Sosaties

Lamb on skewers is a world-wide culinary tradition. In the Far East it's eaten with peanut sauce as Saté, in Turkey as Şiş kebab, in Africa as Sosaties, where it's made from goat as well as lamb. Serve with rice and a good green and oniony salad.

SERVES 4

1 tablespoon oil
1 onion, chopped
1 dessertspoon mild curry powder
250g (8 oz) dried apricots, cooked in a little water until soft
Salt and freshly ground black pepper
500g (1 lb) lamb, cubed (from shoulder or leg)

Heat the oil in a pan and fry the onion until soft. Add the curry powder and fry for 2 minutes. Add the apricots and seasoning and bring to the boil. Remove from the heat, add the lamb and leave to marinate as it cools for 6 hours.

Place the lamb on skewers, packing the cubes tightly together, and grill for 5 minutes on each side.

Heat the marinade until it's boiling again and pour it over the lamb and the rice you're serving it with. It is a wonderful sweet, sour and spicy mixture.

Mediterranean Kebabs

This is one of those recipes that, well done, is superb. When badly done, it takes you back to that taverna somewhere over the wine-dark sea where Zorba's dance was played until 3 o'clock in the morning in a disco that turned out to be right under your window! A nasty dry burnt concoction that made you wonder whether the Greeks did have a word for it. The crafty version should protect you from this.

SERVES 4
2 tablespoons olive oil
2 tablespoons lemon juice
2 cloves of garlic, crushed
1 heaped teaspoon each rosemary and oregano
750g (1½ lb) boned shoulder of lamb, cut into 2.5cm (1 inch) cubes (leg
  would do)
1 each red and green pepper, cored, seeded and cut into 2.5cm (1 inch)
  squares
1 onion, cut into 8 wedges

Mix the oil, lemon juice, garlic and herbs together in a bowl, add the lamb and leave for at least 2 hours to marinate. Thread the skewers, which should have flat sides or be wooden to help in turning the meat, with a piece of red pepper, a piece of meat, a piece of onion, a piece of green pepper, a piece of meat, and so on, until they all are used up. Pack together firmly and do not leave gaps between them. Heat a grill, or a barbecue, to its maximum, place the skewers close to the heat and cook for 3 minutes; turn 45 degrees, cook another 3 minutes, then turn once more and cook for another 3 minutes at most. The meat should be charred on the outside and still succulent on the inside. The vegetables should have blackened on the edges, but not have burned.

CRAFTY TIP

When cooking kebabs, or anything on skewers,
choose wooden or flat sided ones – they enable you
to turn the meat without it slipping, for even
cooking.

Crafty Lamb Breasts

One crafty and cheerful technique uses a breast of lamb (or two) to make the following three dishes at a very economic rate. Buy breasts of lamb, not mutton! Make sure they've not been chopped, though it doesn't hurt if they've been skinned.

Spare Ribs (i)

SERVES 2–4

1 breast of lamb
6 tablespoons soy sauce
6 tablespoons tomato sauce
2 tablespoons brown sugar
4 tablespoons Worcestershire sauce
2 tablespoons lemon juice
1 teaspoon salt
1 dessertspoon made mustard
½ teaspoon each chopped thyme and oregano

Remove the bones from the breast in a sheet. (Keep the meat for the following recipes.) Separate with a sharp knife, making the spare ribs. Blanch in boiling water for 5 minutes, then place in a baking tin. (Keep the water.)

Mix the other ingredients together and pour over the ribs. Cook in a preheated oven, 180°C (350°F) gas mark 4, for 30 minutes, turning them over half way through the cooking time.

Epigrammes of Lamb (ii)

SERVES 4

1 meat-only breast of lamb
1 bay leaf
1 egg, beaten
40g (1½ oz) soft breadcrumbs

Trim off excess fat from one of the reserved 'sheets of lamb' (see above). Place in a large pan of cold water, add the bay leaf, bring to the boil and simmer for 40 minutes. Remove and cool, then cut into oblongs about 5×2.5cm (2×1 inch). Coat in the egg and breadcrumbs, then shallow-fry over a fairly high heat until browned all over. Serve with mashed potatoes.

Apricot-Stuffed Lamb (iii)

SERVES 4

1 meat-only breast of lamb
1 onion, chopped
50g (2 oz) dried apricots, chopped
1 slice bread, soaked in milk
1/2 teaspoon rosemary
Salt and freshly ground black pepper

Trim off excess fat from the remaining 'sheet of lamb' (see page 147).

Mix the onion, apricots and bread together, add the rosemary, and salt and pepper to taste. Spread this mixture on the thicker, narrow end of the lamb, roll it up carefully and tie with string. Cook in a preheated oven, 170°C (325°F) gas mark 3, for 1 hour. Serve with roast potatoes, carrots and gravy.

Lamb Casseroles

Unusual in that lamb is not the most popular meat for casseroling, but these different recipes, two of them French, one Italian and one Persian, have a succulence to them that's ideal for the combination of sweetness and savouriness that is lamb's hallmark.

Baked Lamb Roman-Style

SERVES 4

1 onion, finely chopped and lightly fried
1 tablespoon vinegar or lemon juice
1 teaspoon dried sage
1/2 teaspoon dried rosemary
4 tablespoons tomato paste
1 teaspoon salt
1 teaspoon pepper
1.3 kg (3 lb) shoulder of lamb on the bone, trimmed

Mix all the ingredients together, tossing well to coat the lamb. Bake in a covered casserole in a preheated oven, 170°C (325°F) gas mark 3, for 1 hour, or until the lamb nearly falls off the bone. Remove protruding bones and skim off the excess fat before serving. Serve with long green beans and new or sauté potatoes.

Navarin Printanier

Spring lamb stew is the proper translation of this dish, but I think it's pretty good at any time of the year. The important thing is not to add the vegetables until the meat is nearly done so the whole lot reaches the point of perfection at the same time.

SERVES 4

750g (1½ lb) fillet of lamb, cut into 1 cm (½ inch) pieces
2 tablespoons flour
1 tablespoon vegetable oil
250g (8 oz) button onions
600ml (1 pint) beef stock or water
250g (8 oz) new carrots
250g (8 oz) new potatoes, washed not peeled
1 teaspoon salt
250g (8 oz) button mushrooms
15g (½ oz) butter, melted
1 tablespoon tomato purée
Freshly ground black pepper

Toss the lamb in the flour to coat. Heat the oil in a sauté pan and fry the lamb for 10 minutes, stirring gently. Add the onions and stock and bring to the boil, then simmer for 10 minutes. Add the carrots, potatoes and seasoning, cover and simmer for about 15 minutes, until the potatoes are cooked.

Toss the mushrooms in the melted butter, add to the pan with the tomato purée and heat through for 1 minute. Serve with crusty French bread and a salad to follow.

Ragoût of Lamb Provençale

In the south-west of France, on the edges of Provence, lamb is quite often cooked in a way that resembles the Spanish Basque method, using a lot of red peppers and often a hint of chili. It's an unexpected combination of flavours with lamb but works, I think, remarkably well. It's often served with noodles but is good, too, accompanied by rice and a tossed green salad with plenty of olive oil in the dressing.

SERVES 4
2 tablespoons olive oil
750g (1½ lb) boned shoulder of lamb, cut into 2.5cm (1 inch) pieces
2 onions, chopped
2 large red peppers, cored, seeded and sliced
½ teaspoon each chopped basil and oregano
½ teaspoon chili powder
300ml (½ pint) pasatta
Black olives (optional)
Salt and freshly ground black pepper

Heat the oil in a pan and fry the lamb until it's crisp and brown all over. Add the onion, peppers, herbs and chili powder and stir well. Add the pasatta, season generously and simmer for 35–40 minutes. Add the olives, if you like them, and simmer for 5 minutes.

This dish improves with keeping overnight in the fridge, but make sure it's in an enamel or glass container.

Lamb Polo

This is an example of the rice, meat and fruit dishes that abound throughout the Middle East. It's very similar to the pilaus and birianis that you find to the west and east of it, but the generous use of fruit makes it quite unusual, even in that company.

SERVES 4
25g (1oz) butter
500g (1 lb) boned shoulder of lamb, cut into 2.5cm (1 inch) pieces
1 onion, chopped
1 tablespoon curry powder, or garam masala
½ tablespoon ground coriander
1 teaspoon each turmeric and ground cumin seed
250g (8 oz) can tomatoes
250g (8 oz) dried mixed fruit
250g (8 oz) Basmati or long grain Patna-style rice
Salt and freshly ground black pepper

Melt the butter in a large pan and fry the lamb until lightly brown. Add the onion and the spices and cook, stirring for 2–3 minutes, until the spices give off a fragrant, cooked smell. Stir in the tomatoes, fruit and 600ml (1 pint) boiling water and simmer for 1 hour. Add the rice and enough water to cover the mixture by 2.5cm (1 inch). Bring to the boil, cover and simmer on the gentlest possible heat for 20 minutes, until all the liquid has been absorbed. Season generously. Accompany with yoghurt and chutney.

French Roast Lamb with Garlic and Rosemary

The classic French *gigot d'agneau*, supposedly best made with the lamb from the Breton marshes where it's flavoured by sea marsh herbs. In fact, almost all the *pré-salé* lamb seen in France these days comes from the marshes around Romney in Kent and Sussex. It never reaches the English markets, achieving such a premium price in France, but any good young leg of lamb works equally well.

SERVES 4–6
2 cloves of garlic
1 teaspoon salt
½ teaspoon freshly ground black pepper
1 leg of lamb, trimmed but without the shank being broken
1 dessertspoon rosemary leaves

Crush the garlic with the salt until it makes a smooth purée. Add the pepper and spread the mixture over the lamb rather like you were buttering toast. Sprinkle with the rosemary, rubbed between your hands to break it up a bit first – it will stick to the garlic paste. (Don't be tempted to push chunks of garlic into the lamb, as this only results in little uncooked bits of garlic when you come to eat it.)

Place the lamb on a rack over a roasting tin and pour in about 300ml (½ pint) water. Roast in a preheated oven, 220°C (425°F) gas mark 7, for 20 minutes per 500g (1 lb). Remove from the oven and leave it to rest in a warm place for 5 minutes per 500g (1 lb): if it's a 1.75kg (4 lb) leg of lamb this means 20 minutes. Don't worry, it won't get cold – it'll just continue to cook a little from its own heat but, most important of all, absorb its own juice and become extremely tender to carve.

The juices that flow from it when you carve should be mixed with the gravy in the bottom of the pan and served, without any thickening, with the lamb. Pommes de Terre Dauphinoise (see page 173) and spinach are the classic accompaniments.

Welsh Roast Lamb

This is a recipe from my Welsh childhood, combining a flavouring of honey – unexpected but superb with the lamb – and cooking the vegetables under the meat, an old British custom we tend to have forgotten except on the Celtic fringes. You can use either a leg or a shoulder for this dish. The shoulder, which is a fattier cut, makes the vegetables a little greasy for my taste, but if you drain the fat from them before eating, the flavour is superb.

SERVES 4–6

1 kg (2 lb) potatoes, sliced
750g (1½ lb) onions, sliced
1 leg or part-boned shoulder of lamb
2 tablespoons clear honey
Handful of fresh mint, chopped
Salt and freshly ground black pepper

Layer the potatoes and onions in a roasting tin or dish and season generously. Place the lamb on a rack over the vegetables and roast in a preheated oven, 220°C (425°F) gas mark 7, for 10 minutes per 500g (1 lb). Season generously, turn fat side uppermost and spread with the honey, making sure it covers as much of the upper surface as you can manage. Sprinkle the mint over the vegetables. Cook for another 10 minutes per 500g (1 lb). Remove the joint from the oven and keep warm for 20 minutes. Drain any excess juices from the vegetables, cover and keep warm. Make sure everyone gets a slice of the vegetable layer with their lamb.

CRAFTY TIP

When roasting meat, leave it to 'rest' for at least 10 minutes before carving. This allows the joint to absorb it own juices and tenderise itself.

Offal isn't awful

A few recipes to demonstrate that the bits of animals we tend to regard with distaste *can* taste absolutely delicious.

Clubman's Kidneys

As well as having a lot of strange customs like refusing ladies membership, the gentlemen's clubs of Pall Mall were renowned for their very fine cooking. This rich, very simple dish, which was developed in clubland, is in that tradition of masculine cooking that women can at least share.

SERVES 4

12 lambs' kidneys
75g (3 oz) butter
1 tablespoon prepared mustard
2 tablespoons Worcestershire sauce
4 tablespoons tomato sauce
2 tablespoons chutney
300ml (½ pint) beef stock

Clean, skin and split the kidneys in half and remove the cores. Melt the butter in a pan and fry the kidneys gently for 5 minutes. Add the mustard, sauces and chutney and stir for 1 minute. Increase the heat and add the stock. Stir and simmer for 5 minutes.

Serve on fried bread with mashed potatoes, carrots and parsnips.

Liver Venetian Style

This dish needs a little faith to try it, as its cooking method is hardly orthodox. Nevertheless, it's one of the most delicious ways of cooking liver.

SERVES 4

1 tablespoon vegetable oil
2 onions, thinly sliced
2 tablespoons chopped parsley
6 tablespoons water
1 tablespoon cider or wine vinegar
500g (1 lb) lambs' liver, very thinly sliced

Heat the oil in a wide pan and fry the onions for 5 minutes, until soft but not brown. Add the parsley, water and vinegar and bring to the boil. Add the liver and cook quickly, turning once, for 2–3 minutes only. Serve the liver with the onions on top and with rice mixed with green peas (called Risi Bisi in Venice).

CRAFTY TIP

Calves' and lambs' liver can be used almost interchangeably, though calves' has the more delicate taste (and price). The important thing is to get either cut well – regular, even slices, not hacked into chunks. If necessary, buy it in one piece and cut it up yourself, 1 cm (½ inch) thick and across the grain. Use the trimmings for pâté.

Flash Fried Liver

One of the simplest and craftiest of dishes this one, though never seen or broadcast about before to the best of my knowledge. It's a family favourite that will convert even liver haters. The important thing is not to overcook – believe the timings and try them. You can use calves' or lambs' liver, but make sure it's cut in even slices approximately 1cm (½ inch) thick and make sure it's the freshest, best liver you can buy. Have the plates hot and the vegetables ready – you are a minute-and-a-half away from your main course.

SERVES 4

1 tablespoon peanut or sunflower oil
500g (1 lb) liver
4 tablespoons flour
50g (2 oz) butter
1 tablespoon chopped herbs (parsley, chives, sage, tarragon or oregano)
   or 1 dessertspoon dried herbs (as above)
Salt and freshly ground black pepper

Choose a heavy-based frying pan, big enough to take all the liver at once or in 2 batches. Have a warm serving dish ready.

   Heat the pan until very hot, then grease with the oil. Rub the liver with the flour and place in the hot pan, pressing down with a spatula. Cook for 30 seconds on one side, turn and cook for 45 seconds on the other side. Remove to the warm plate. Cook the second batch of liver if necessary.

Add the butter to the pan and allow it to foam, then add the herbs and swirl round. Season the liver with salt and a little pepper, pour over the herb butter and serve immediately.

Oxtail Casserole

This recipe has proved one of the most successful ever for the *Food and Drink* programme. We were told by Smithfield that within three days of the recipe being broadcast Britain had run out of oxtails. If they've arrived again since then in your butchers, ask for one and try it. It's a very rich casserole with a hint of the Mediterranean because this particular recipe has the garnish that's traditionally added in Italy to an osso bucco stew. It's made of freshly chopped garlic, lemon rind and parsley and called a *gremolata*. Even if you're not a garlic lover, you'll find that the combination of flavours and piquancy that this adds to the long simmered stew is really worth trying.

SERVES 4
2 tablespoons olive oil
1 kg (2 lb) oxtail, cut into 2.5 cm (1 inch) slices
250g (8 oz) onions, chopped
1 clove of garlic, finely chopped
500ml (18 fl oz) pasatta or approximately 1½ cans chopped tomatoes
*   (to make up same volume)*
½ teaspoon each dried oregano, thyme and basil
Salt and freshly ground black pepper

FOR THE GARNISH:
2 cloves of garlic, finely chopped
Grated rind of 1 lemon
2 tablespoons chopped parsley

Heat the oil in a large pan and fry the oxtail pieces until browned. Add the onions, garlic, pasatta or chopped tomatoes, herbs and seasoning to taste. Cover and simmer for 4 hours, either on top of the stove or, preferably, in a preheated oven, 170°C (325°F) gas mark 3. Check the dish at regular intervals to ensure that it stays moist; if it starts to dry out, add a little water.

Transfer to an oval serving dish, or serve on a bed of long grain rice coloured with saffron if you wish.

Mix the garnish ingredients together and sprinkle over the oxtail.

Green and Pleasant . . .

The most universally accepted change in cooking over the last fifteen years has been the move towards *crisp* vegetables. There are those who have taken this even to the extreme of considering crisp potatoes – the insides I mean, not the outsides. But leaving eccentricities aside, wherever you go from Cardiff back street to Clapham High Street, from family kitchen to restaurant table, there is general agreement that carrots and cabbage, cauliflower and beans should all have a crispness, a little bite left to them when they're cooked and served. Not only is it the most widespread of the recent cooking revolutions, it is also, for me, the most welcome.

Vegetables have played a central part in crafty cooking since the beginning and more and more in recent years as people's taste for meat has declined and vegetables have taken centre stage.

Cooked properly and flavoured in a variety of simple but complementary ways, vegetables don't need an apology if served alone. We often serve them at home in groups of four or five dishes, forgetting about meat entirely, and have never yet had anybody raise a voice of complaint. Contrasts of texture and colour, as well as flavour and sharpness, are important, and often very simply achieved.

Rather than giving individual recipes, I've written a section on each of my favourite vegetables with ideas, hints, observations and specific cooking methods mixed together.

A selection of crafty salads completes the chapter, ranging from elaborate to very simple confections. Salads have always been a central part of 'crafty' cooking, very rarely as a side dish, but rather on their own. One of the exceptions to this is the most spectacular salad of all – Salad Elana, made with strawberries and cucumbers. There is simply nothing like it eaten with a freshly poached, cold whole salmon.

Artichokes

Globe

Use one artichoke for each person. Trim the tops of the leaves so they are level and cut the stalk off flush at the base. Place in a pan of acidulated (1 teaspoon lemon juice or vinegar per artichoke) boiling water and boil for 20 minutes. Remove the centre, the bud-like tightly folded leaves and the funny 'choke' under it, using a sharp spoon or a knife, and serve hot with Hollandaise Sauce (see page 24) or melted butter, or cold with a good garlicky mayonnaise. If the artichoke's centre has come away cleanly, it's quite clever to use the artichoke itself as a cup for the sauce. Simply pull off the leaves in succession from round the edge and dip in the sauce. Eat the succulent base of the leaves.

Jerusalem

These look like knobbly potatoes. They're quite difficult to peel but these days the silver-skinned varieties don't need peeling, they just need scrubbing. They have a lovely hazelnutty flavour and mash down to produce some delicious purées, but for complex chemical reasons they're not nearly as fattening as potatoes. Try a purée of equal parts of potatoes, Jerusalem artichokes and celeriac mashed with butter, salt and pepper.

Jerusalem Artichokes Provençal

SERVES 4

2 tablespoons olive oil
500g (1 lb) Jerusalem artichokes (scrubbed but not peeled), cut into
    5mm (1/4 inch) slices
1 onion, finely chopped
1 clove of garlic crushed with 1 teaspoon salt
2 tablespoons tomato purée

Heat the oil in a deep frying pan and sauté the artichokes for 5 minutes on each side. Stir in the onion and garlic salt, then add the tomato purée and just enough water to make the dish moist. Cook over a low heat for 20–25 minutes, until the sauce is really thick. Stir the artichokes through the sauce to coat them all evenly before serving.

Asparagus

Asparagus has only a brief season, which should be relished. To prepare, simply scrub and peel the base of the stalks with a potato peeler and cook in a pan of boiling water, with the heads *out* of the water, for 12–15 minutes, until tender. Serve hot with top quality melted butter with a third of its volume in lemon juice mixed in, or the very best Hollandaise Sauce (see page 24). Alternatively, serve cold with mayonnaise. Use nothing but your fingers to eat it with.

Beans

I love beans of almost all sorts. The recipes for some dried bean dishes are in Chapter 5 but the fresh green beans, runner or stringless French, are among my favourite vegetables. I rarely do runner beans by any method other than the way my grandmother used to cook them in Wales, for my mother and then for me. The method is simplicity itself and, served with some good bread and butter, makes a complete light meal.

Top, tail and string (if necessary) good quality runner beans, then cut into 5mm (¼ inch) slices diagonally across the grain. Plunge into boiling water for just 8 minutes, until they are still bright green and a little crunchy, but cooked through. Serve in individual bowls with a large knob of salted butter and sprinkle lots of freshly ground black pepper and chopped parsley on the top. Have plenty of bread and butter in the middle of the table and you won't hear a sound until the bowls are empty.

Beans Almondine

For the rather more refined French beans that don't need stringing, here is my favourite method which, with a slight variation, was picked up in the depths of the Chinese quarter of Soho late one night.

SERVES 4
500g (1 lb) stringless French beans
25g (1 oz) butter
50g (2 oz) slivered almonds
Salt and freshly ground black pepper

Top and tail the beans and cook in a saucepan of boiling water for 8 minutes. Drain and rinse quickly under cold running water. Melt the butter in the emptied pan, add the almonds and fry until they're just turning the very palest gold. Add the beans, cover the pan and give it a shake for just 1 minute over a moderate heat. Season to taste, tip out and serve. The beans will have absorbed the buttery juices and the almonds will still be crisp.

CHINESE VARIATION

Use 3 plump thinly sliced cloves of garlic and 1 tablespoon cooking oil (not olive oil) instead of the almonds and butter. The method is exactly the same, the result surprisingly different, but despite the amount of garlic, not intolerably pungent.

Beetroot

Despite the terrible tendency we have to put beetroot in malt vinegar, it can be a very delicate vegetable. It is used to make marvellous soups in central Europe, usually called by a name which includes the word borstch, but in America they make the two ultimate beetroot dishes:

Harvard Beets

Cut cooked beetroot into 1cm (½ inch) cubes. Heat it gently in a pan with a knob of butter and, when really hot, add 2 tablespoons each double and soured cream for every 250g (8 oz) beetroot. Stir very quickly and serve hot. The combination of bright red beetroot and pink-tinged cream, of sweet and sour, is delicious and goes particularly well with grilled meats.

Red Flannel Hash

Invented, perhaps, in a moment of desperation when there were no potatoes, this is a classic from the mid-west. Sauté a thinly sliced onion with a can of corned beef, mashed up. Add 500g (1 lb) peeled and grated cooked beetroot, mix thoroughly together, season with black pepper, and sauté until there's a thin crust on the pancake-like mixture. Serve with poached or fried eggs, if you wish. Although it may sound outlandish, it tastes delicious.

Broccoli

I think it was Elizabeth David who said that broccoli got cold faster than any other vegetable she'd ever known. That is certainly true. It also goes khaki-coloured faster than any *I've* known! The trick with cooking it is to steam it if you can, either in a proper Chinese-type basket steamer or in one that goes inside saucepans and unfolds like a flower or, if necessary, in a colander over a little boiling water in a saucepan, with the lid on.

Trim the florets until they're all about an even size and steam for not more than 8 minutes, so they are bright green, still crisp but tender. You can 'cheese sauce' them or, if you're feeling a little exotic, sprinkle a little sesame oil and good soy sauce on them, or you can pour a little melted butter, in which you have fried slivered almonds to a golden brown, over them. Whatever you do, serve them on hot plates very quickly.

CRAFTY TIP

Never add bicarbonate of soda to the water when boiling green vegetables to help retain their colour. It destroys their vitamin C content. Simply cook them slightly less – until tender but still crisp.

Brussels Sprouts

Another of the great under-rated vegetables – not surprising when you see the khaki-coloured, solid bullets that are often served as representatives of this vegetable. The recipes that follow are anything but canteen food and certainly the Polonaise stands on its own as a separate vegetable course. Sprouts also make delicious soup as long as they've not been overcooked in the first place.

Salade Niçoise (below)
Salad Elana (left)

Apricot Tart

Sprouts Polonaise

The key thing is not to overcook the sprouts. The combination of bright green nutty vegetables, slightly garlicky breadcrumbs and the soft lightness the chopped eggs bring, make it a really unexpected treat.

SERVES 4
500g (1 lb) Brussels sprouts
50g (2 oz) butter
40g (1½ oz) fresh breadcrumbs
1 teaspoon garlic salt
2 hard-boiled eggs

Cook the sprouts in boiling water for 8 minutes. Drain well. Melt half the butter in a pan and fry the breadcrumbs until brown. Add the garlic salt. Reserve the yolks of the hard-boiled eggs and chop the whites. Melt the rest of the butter in a frying pan, add the sprouts and sizzle for 1 minute. Add the breadcrumbs and chopped egg whites, turn into a serving dish and cover with the crumbled egg yolks. Serve with plenty of freshly ground black pepper.

Sprout Purée

This is the ideal answer if the sprouts are a bit 'leggy' but still worth cooking. You can use a food processor but there are those (including my wife) who prefer the texture you get with a little hard work and a large sharp knife.

SERVES 4
500g (1 lb) Brussels sprouts
1 small onion, chopped
50g (2 oz) butter
Salt and freshly ground black pepper

Cook the sprouts, with the onion, in boiling water for 8–10 minutes, until they're still bright green but quite soft. Drain and purée in a food processor or blender, or chop very finely with a really sharp knife. Add the butter, plenty of black pepper and salt to taste and stir over a low heat until fairly smooth and creamy. It needs a good strong dish to eat with it, but the flavour is remarkable.

Cabbage

Crafty Cabbage

This is the quickest and simplest of all cabbage recipes and, without question, the best. It's a kind of *shake* rather than stir fry and can be adapted to other green vegetables like spring or Cornish greens as well. It's not, however, a recipe for the type of hard Dutch cabbage you use for coleslaw. Vegetables that cook best in this way have a strong tint of green about them.

SERVES 4–6
750g (1½ lb) green cabbage
300ml (½ pint) water
25g (1 oz) butter
Salt and freshly ground black pepper

Core the cabbage and discard any broken or damaged leaves. Cut across the grain into 1cm (½ inch) ribbons. Place the water and butter in a saucepan, which will take all the cabbage at once and has a good fitting lid, and bring to the boil. When the water has boiled and the butter has melted, add all the cabbage and season generously. Cover the pan, shake vigorously and cook on maximum heat for 1 minute. Shake again, holding on the lid with your hand wrapped in a tea towel, return to the heat for 45 seconds, then serve.

The cabbage will be buttery, crisp and cooked through, having steamed in its own juices. Don't be tempted to do anything else except season it generously with plenty of black pepper and a good pinch of salt.

Red Cabbage

The best way of cooking red cabbage is to make a casserole of it in its own right. It's a German or Hungarian tradition, which varies from area to area and region to region. I think that this version, very simple to make and taking quite a little while to cook, is one of the best. It's a dish that will reheat with advantage the next day. Don't worry about the colour – it will go a deep dark maroon that will flatter most dishes, particularly the kind of rich game or grills that it goes best with.

SERVES 4
1 tablespoon oil
1 small red cabbage, shredded
1 large onion, sliced
1 large cooking apple, cored and chopped
2 tablespoons each brown sugar and malt vinegar
Salt and freshly ground black pepper

Heat the oil in a large saucepan or flameproof casserole. Add the cabbage and onion and fry for 5 minutes. Add the other ingredients, stir well, then just cover with water. Cover the pan and simmer for 45 minutes. Check the seasoning and serve.

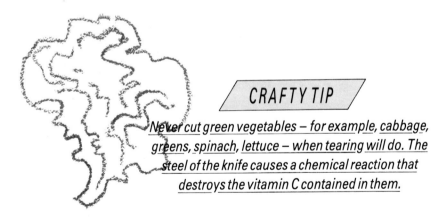

CRAFTY TIP

Never cut green vegetables – for example, cabbage, greens, spinach, lettuce – when tearing will do. The steel of the knife causes a chemical reaction that destroys the vitamin C contained in them.

Carrots

The French think they're the only people who know how to cook carrots. They're wrong, because the Chinese do too and, interestingly enough, use a very similar technique. The basic difference is in the way that they cut the carrots and the way that they flavour them, as these two recipes show.

Carrots Vichy

The theory is that Carrots Vichy are so named because the water which has become famous in its bottled version from around the town of Vichy is the best there is for cooking carrots. The other ingredients are very simple, but good carrots are *essential*. If you can find organically grown ones the reward is enormous. Of all organically grown vegetables, I think carrots show the biggest improvement from the normal additive-grown versions.

SERVES 4
500g (1 lb) carrots
25g (1 oz) butter
1 teaspoon sugar
½ teaspoon salt
250ml (8 fl oz) water

Cut the carrots crossways on a slight bias into 5mm (¼ inch) slices. (If they're very tiny, cut them into quarters lengthways.) Place in a pan, add the butter, sugar and salt and just enough water to come level with the top of the carrots when they're shaken down – don't be tempted to add more. Bring to the boil and cook at a fast simmer for 8–10 minutes. The water should virtually all evaporate and the carrots should wind up bathed in a buttery, slightly sugary, caramelised sauce.

When you serve them, tip the sauce out with them if the water's all gone; if not, remove the carrots, then boil the liquid until you've only got the syrup left and pour that over the carrots. The flavour is absolutely delicious.

Chinese Aniseed Carrots

This Chinese method of cooking is known as stir-braising. It is a very quick way of cooking a hard root vegetable. The Chinese way of cutting the carrots is designed to make sure that all the pieces have the maximum surface area for their volume and to ensure they all cook at about the same speed.

SERVES 4
500g (1 lb) carrots
1 tablespoon soy sauce
½ teaspoon star anise pieces (not powder)
Pinch each salt and sugar
120 ml (4 fl oz) water

To cut the carrots Chinese-style: place the carrot in front of you, pointing it across you. Hold the knife at 45 degrees to the carrot and cut down 1cm (½ inch) from the end. Roll the carrot a quarter turn towards you so that the diagonal cut now faces upwards. Bring the knife down again in the same way. You will find yourself cutting little triangular sections of carrot, rather like mini pyramids.

Place all the cut carrots in a pan, add the soy sauce, star anise, salt and sugar and enough water to come just level with the top of the carrots. Bring to a fast boil, cover and give them a good shake, then boil for 8 minutes, by which time all the water should have evaporated, leaving the carrots dark honey-brown and strongly flavoured. Discard the star anise and serve as a vegetable with grilled meats or fish, or as part of a Chinese dinner.

Cauliflower

The much-maligned cauliflower is a wonderful vegetable that people in other countries seem to regard more highly than we do. A good cauliflower cheese can be great provided the cauliflower isn't overcooked to begin with.

Break the cauliflower into florets and cook in boiling water for about 2 minutes. Drain well, place in an ovenproof dish and cover with a good rich cheese sauce (see page 23). Bake in a preheated oven, 200°C (400°F) gas mark 6, for about 15 minutes. This allows the cauliflower to finish cooking under the sauce, rather than to be cooked before the sauce is added.

A lightly cooked cauliflower is delicious too if it's left to cool, broken into large chunks and served with a vinaigrette or lemonette dressing poured over it. Chopped parsley and chives can be sprinkled over the top. Don't forget cauliflower soup. Make it with an onion and with equal quantities of milk and water, saving a couple of the florets. Liquidise with the uncooked florets that you've kept back – a creamy soup with a crunchy texture.

Cauliflower can also be cooked 'Polonaise' (see page 160 – using cauliflower florets instead of sprouts).

Celeriac

Europe's answer to our passion for celery – a bulbous vegetable with exactly the same flavour and a totally different texture. The two best ways of eating it, despite the French propensity for making it into a raw salad, are boiled and served under a cheese sauce in a gratin, and in a hot purée, with Jerusalem artichokes (see page 157).

Celery

Celery is best eaten raw as in a Waldorf Salad (see page 114) or, sliced across the grain diagonally, in a stir fry. Celery makes a good flavouring to soup but not as the central ingredient – it's too stringy to give a good texture. It's nice mixed into a hot potato salad or served with soured cream for jacket potatoes. I like it as an edible 'swizzle' stick in a tall glass of well seasoned tomato juice.

Courgettes

Courgettes are now a culinary cliché, but twenty years ago I remember the first of them coming to Britain, largely due to the campaigning of that doyenne of cookery writers and food experts, Elizabeth David. Tiny marrows were unheard of in the 1950s and, when they arrived, we cooked them in all sorts of ways, including the most complicated sweet and sour Italian recipes and with Provençal stuffings.

After years of experimentation, my view is that there are just three ways of cooking courgettes to their best, and only two of those are ones I'd care to try at home. There is no question that Zucchini Fritti – tiny slivers of courgette dipped in a crisp batter and deep-fried – are one of the triumphs of Italian cooking, but I'm not a great deep-fryer, you see. My two methods don't need pints of hot oil with all the trouble and smells that go with it and, therefore, are much more suited to crafty cooking.

Shake-Fried Courgettes Provençal

SERVES 4
500g (1 lb) courgettes
2 tablespoons olive oil
½ teaspoon garlic salt (or salt crushed with a clove of garlic)
1 tablespoon tomato purée

Slice the courgettes into 5mm (¼ inch) rounds just before you are ready to cook them. Heat the oil in a large pan until it's just starting to smoke. Add the courgettes and garlic salt, cover and give it a thorough shake. Leave for 30 seconds. Add the tomato purée, cover and shake again and leave for 45 seconds. Serve immediately.

Incredibly, the courgettes will have absorbed the garlic, tomato and olive oil flavours, be steaming hot in their own juices, still crisp and absolutely superb.

Steamed Courgettes

This is a very simple and highly digestible way of eating the delicious vegetable. If you have fresh crisp courgettes, it brings out all their flavour.

SERVES 4
500g (1 lb) courgettes
25g (1 oz) butter
Salt and freshly ground black pepper

Semi-peel the courgettes, using a fine potato peeler to take off sections lengthways, leaving ridges of peel around the courgette. The central reason for this is decorative. Cut the courgettes into 2.5cm (1 inch) pieces, place in a colander and sprinkle with 2 tablespoons salt. Leave for 10 minutes for the bitter juices to be drawn out, rinse thoroughly, then place in a steamer (or the colander again) over a pan containing about 5cm (2 inches) boiling water. Cover and steam for just 5 minutes.

Melt the butter in a clean pan, without browning, roll the courgettes in it and leave over a very low heat for 1 minute, for the vegetables to absorb the butter. Season to taste and serve immediately.

Fennel

Fennel looks like fat celery – slice it across the grain and use in the same way. It has a decidedly aniseedy flavour and lends itself to most of the dishes celery can be used for, including eating raw. It makes a wonderful ingredient for a stir fry, particularly with a bunch of spring onions and a red pepper to add colour contrast to its very pale green.

Leeks

Leeks are one of the oldest vegetables we know. They were used as a flavouring in food all over the ancient world. Our current image of them as khaki mush is another legacy of the school dinner method of cooking that appears to have grown up since the last war. Forget it and enjoy one of the most flavourful of the winter's crops. *Crisply* cooked they are even scrumptious coated with a white sauce. Just remember to wash them really thoroughly and not to cook them too long.

CRAFTY TIP

After initial thorough washing, place sliced leeks in a bowl of cold water. Press them down and keep them under the water with a saucepan or plate. Leave for at least 30 minutes, to remove all grit and sand.

Leeks in White Sauce

Although this is another of those 'school food' horrors, fresh leeks, poached to perfection and covered with a good white sauce, are a real winter pleasure. Discovered about four years ago in a Welsh restaurant that specialised in vegetables, it has now become a dinner party regular in my house. Do be sure to wash the leeks really thoroughly to remove all the grit that gets between the leaves.

SERVES 4
750g (1½ lb) leeks, cut into 2.5cm (1 inch) lengths
1 quantity White Sauce (see page 23)

Place the leeks in a saucepan half-filled with boiling water, cover and cook for just 5 minutes. Drain immediately and mix into the hot white sauce. Place in a gratin dish and flash them under a hot grill for not more than a couple of minutes, so the top just browns and bubbles a little.

Serve with other food or as a marvellous starter on their own. A pinch of nutmeg in the white sauce is a good addition.

Peppers

Peppers came to us, as did so much that is delicious, from the New World. There they formed a staple part of the diet of the civilisations that lived in what is now Mexico. The people grew a vast variety of peppers – hot, spicy, and sweet – they still do though we tend to get only a very few kinds here. This situation is improving with the arrival of yellow and black ones and a couple of kinds of chili pepper (they are not all murderous by the way, some are just spicy). Try using peppers raw as dip 'scoopers', or cut in half and filled with seasoned rice, or with grated cheese and onion, before baking in the oven. If you are using them for a salad, either grill them first and rub off as much of the waxy coating as you can, or fry them quickly for 2 minutes in the oil that you were going to use in the dressing – then add the rest of the dressing when they are cool.

Stuffed Peppers

You can make this dish with leftover rice if you have any, but it's worth specially boiling rice for it. This makes a smashing starter for four, or a light main course, served with a tomato salad and crusty bread, for two.

SERVES 2 OR 4
2 large red or green peppers
125g (4 oz) long grain rice, boiled for 10 minutes and rinsed
175g (6 oz) cheese, grated
1 onion, chopped
1 clove of garlic, finely chopped
2 tablespoons chopped herbs (I like oregano and sage)
2 tablespoons pine nuts
Pinch of chili powder
Salt and freshly ground black pepper

Split the peppers lengthways and remove the core and seeds. Mix the rice, 150 g (5 oz) of the cheese, the onion, garlic, herbs and nuts together. Season highly with salt and pepper and a little chili powder. Add a little water if the mixture is very dry. Fill the peppers with the mixture, top with the reserved cheese and bake in a preheated oven, 200°C (400°F) gas mark 6, for 30 minutes. Cover with foil if they start to burn on top.

CRAFTY TIP

If you find peppers slightly indigestible, removing their skins helps: place them under a very hot grill, as close to the heat as possible, until the skin is black and charred on all sides. Rub off the skins under cold running water.

Petits Pois

Good fresh peas are a rarity these days unless you grow them yourself. Frozen ones are good for soups or stir fry dishes or for this French concoction.

Petits Pois Français

Even with frozen peas, this little vegetable recipe is a pleasure – if you can get fresh petits pois it's that much more delicious. Despite the belief that French canned petits pois are worth eating, I'm afraid it's a habit I've never caught, so if you can't buy fresh or frozen peas to do this with, just don't bother. The dish has the added virtue of making quite a small quantity of peas go a long way and using up the bits of the lettuce that otherwise normally get thrown away.

SERVES 4–6
50g (2 oz) butter
6 outside lettuce leaves, cut into 5mm (¼ inch) ribbons
6 spring onions, thinly sliced (green and white parts)
500g (1 lb) petits pois (or ordinary peas)
4 tablespoons cold water

Melt the butter in a moderate size saucepan, add the lettuce, onion, peas and water. If using fresh peas, cover and simmer for 8 minutes; if using frozen, cover and bring quickly to the boil, then remove from heat. Season and serve.

If it's worked properly there should be a little buttery liquid in the bottom of the pan.

Potatoes

There are more ways of cooking a potato and more kinds of potato to cook than almost any other vegetable. This is not an attempt at a comprehensive guide, just a few thoughts on the kinds of potatoes to use and the best way to cook the all-time favourites, plus a couple of recipes.

There are really two kinds of potato worth considering. The waxy kind that don't fall apart very easily – Jersey Royals and the newly available Fir Apple Pink and Kipfler – are marvellous for sautéing, salads and the sliced potato dishes you'll find on pages 172–3. The other kind make the best roast potatoes, chips and mashed potatoes – King Edwards are the most famous but now, because of EEC rules, there are a whole range of other ones. The red-skinned Desirées make wonderful roast potatoes.

Mashed Potatoes. The secret with these is to cook them until they are really soft, drain them thoroughly, then return to the heat to dry a little. Add *hot* milk, not cold, a good knob of butter and some nutmeg or celery salt, then mash. When you've finishing mashing, the trick is to whip the potatoes with a whisk or an electric beater, or if you're feeling very brave, with a fork until your hand aches. The potatoes will go light, white and fluffy and the transformation is quite worth the effort.

Roast potatoes. The secret here is to blanch them first. Cut the potatoes into even sized pieces, bring to the boil in salted water and boil for not more than 8 minutes, then drain well. While they're cooking, put a couple of tablespoons of oil into a roasting pan and place in a preheated oven, 190°C (375°F) gas mark 5, until it is really hot. Roll the potatoes thoroughly in the oil and roast in the oven for 35–40 minutes, until they're golden and crispy. Roll them over at least once. You can roast parsnips in exactly the same way – they're wonderful.

Chips. Though I'm not a deep fryer, the trick if you are cooking chips is to cook them twice: once until they are pale gold, then drain, turn the heat up and refry for 45 seconds. The chips will be snapping crisp.

CRAFTY TIP

To speed up the cooking time for jacket potatoes, cook them on metal skewers. Use the long kebab type and pierce through the widest part of the potato ('lengthways'). You should get two potatoes per skewer. The metal absorbs the heat and passes it into the centre of the potato.

Pommes de Terre Anna

This very simple dish is really a kind of fried potato cake, which is particularly good with grilled meats or even a midweek sausage. It should be served like a cake, too, cut in wedges.

SERVES 4–6

4 tablespoons oil
750g (1½ lb) potatoes, cut into 5mm (¼ inch) slices
25g (1 oz) butter
Salt and freshly ground black pepper

Heat half the oil in a frying pan into which the potato will fit in about 3 layers, until it's sizzling hot. Remove from the heat and very carefully layer the potatoes in the pan, pressing down with a spatula and seasoning as you go.

Lower the heat, return the potatoes and cook for 15 minutes, giving the occasional shake. The potatoes will start to set into a solid unit. Remove from the heat, put a plate over the pan, invert the plate and pan together, then slide the potato cake, raw-side down, back into the pan. Pour the remaining oil around the edge of the pan so it runs under the cake and add the butter, cut into 4 pieces. Give it all a good shake and leave it to cook for another 10 minutes, until the underside is equally brown. Invert onto a plate again, cut into wedges and serve.

Pommes de Terre Dauphinoise

This is the most luxurious of potato dishes. In France it's traditionally served with luxury meats like grilled calves' liver or gigot of lamb. The dish is so rich and delicious that I enjoy eating it very much on its own, or with a couple of other vegetable dishes as a vegetarian meal. It's got quite a lot of cream in it, but when you think about it, the cream is rather better put to use here than poured over fruit, which probably doesn't need it and whose flavour is impaired by it. The cream blends most wonderfully with the potato and only adds up to about a tablespoon of double cream per person.

SERVES 4
750g (1½ lb) firm potatoes (Desirée or King Edwards are best), cut into
    5mm (¼ inch) slices
1 clove of garlic, peeled and cut in half
50g (2 oz) butter
Salt and freshly ground black pepper
150ml (¼ pint) each double cream and milk, mixed together

After peeling and slicing the potatoes, there is much debate whether or not to wash them again. I have tried both ways and find the dish made with unwashed potato slices slightly heavier. (The washing simply removes some of the starch from the potatoes and makes the overall finished dish lighter.) Either way, take an earthenware dish about 3.5–4cm (1½ inches) deep and rub it with the pieces of garlic. Allow the garlic juices to dry and then rub the dish with half the butter.

Arrange the potatoes in layers, sprinkling salt and pepper and the remaining butter over them as you go. When you've finished, pour over the cream and milk. Cover lightly with a piece of foil or buttered paper and place in a preheated oven, 200°C (400°F) gas mark 6, for 30 minutes. Take off the buttered paper or foil and leave to cook for another 25–30 minutes, until the top is thoroughly golden brown and the whole thing is bubbling and juicy.

Ratatouille

Perhaps the most famous of all the vegetable dishes to come out of France. The secret is not to cook the vegetables too long, so they retain their individual flavours and textures while blending into a delicious whole. For close friends, try adding a little extra garlic. It can be served cold as a starter for six, hot as an accompaniment for four–six, or hot with crusty French bread as a light lunch or supper for four.

SERVES 4–6

6 tablespoons vegetable oil (olive if possible)
1 clove of garlic, chopped
250g (8 oz) each aubergines, courgettes and onions, thinly sliced
250g (8 oz) red or green peppers, cored, seeded and thinly sliced
400g (14 oz) can tomatoes, drained
Salt and freshly ground black pepper

Heat the oil in a large pan and fry the garlic for 1 minute. Add the prepared vegetables and cook, stirring, for 5 minutes. Add the tomatoes and cook gently for 30 minutes, without covering, stirring occasionally. Season highly and serve as above.

Spinach

For years and years and years, as a child, I loathed spinach! It's taken a few years as an adult to come to appreciate the full deliciousness of this vegetable. The following two recipes are really the main reason for my conversion. They're essentially similar in style, but surprisingly different in taste because of the flavouring additions. Don't forget to wash the spinach thoroughly.

Don't be frightened of the one with orange, by the way. Unlikely and outlandish as it sounds, it works a treat. In the eighteenth century, spinach was often used in English cooking as a sweet rather than a savoury ingredient in pies and puddings. This recipe is entirely savoury in intent, but the hint of sweetness brings out the flavour of the spinach marvellously.

Spinach with Orange

SERVES 4

750g (1½ lb) spinach
50g (2 oz) butter
Juice of 1 orange
½ teaspoon salt
Freshly ground black pepper (optional)

Plunge the spinach into your largest saucepan half-filled with boiling water. (Be careful!) As soon as the spinach has softened, which will take about 1½ minutes, drain it very thoroughly in a colander, cutting across it with a sharp knife to get rid of all the liquid you can. Melt the butter in the cleaned pan, add the spinach and turn it a couple of times, then add the orange juice. Cook for about 2 minutes, season with salt and, if you like, with black pepper.

It's traditionally served with small triangles of fried bread – a lovely crisp addition to the rich green succulence of the spinach.

Creamed Spinach

The effect of milk or cream on spinach is supposedly to get rid of the unpleasant bitterness of the oxalic acid present in it. I've never noticed it in fresh spinach myself, but it's said to be much better for your health and better for your digestion cooked like this.

SERVES 4

750g (1½ lb) spinach
25g (1 oz) butter
4 tablespoons double cream or fromage frais
Salt and freshly ground black pepper

Plunge the spinach into your largest saucepan half-filled with boiling water. Leave it to soften for about 2 minutes, then drain thoroughly in a colander, cutting across it with a knife to help the liquid run out. Leave it to stand for 1–2 minutes. Melt the butter in the cleaned pan, add the spinach and season generously. Add the cream or fromage frais and stir together, allowing the spinach to heat through but not to come to the boil.

To serve, fork the spinach up a little and dribble a drop more cream (or fromage frais) in the centre, just to give it a slightly marbled effect.

Super Salads

Brown Rice Salad

This is one to experiment with, and perhaps offer to vegetarian friends. However, even meat-eaters like the combination of nutty rice and crunchy bits with a sharp lemony dressing. Made in sufficient quantity it can also be the basis for a summer barbecue salad. Although you can eat this dish hot or cold, I prefer it cold.

SERVES 4
250g (8 oz) brown rice
1 cucumber, deseeded and diced
4 celery sticks, chopped
8 radishes, sliced

OPTIONAL ADDITIONS:
Pineapple cubes
Diced eating apple
Shelled walnuts
Cooked vegetables

FOR THE DRESSING:
2 tablespoons lemon juice
4 tablespoons salad oil
1 teaspoon each brown sugar, garlic salt and prepared mustard

Cook the rice in plenty of boiling salted water, covered, for 30–40 minutes, stirring occasionally, until tender. Drain carefully and rinse in hot water.

Whisk all the dressing ingredients together in a bowl and add the rice while it's still warm, tossing well. Leave to cool, then mix in the cucumber, celery and radishes and any of the suggested additions you like. Leave for at least 30 minutes, to let the flavours blend.

Serve as a first course, or as a main course with other salads.

Salade Niçoise

On the salad front, this is France's great claim to fame (apart from vinaigrette). It comes, as its name suggests, from the area around Nice in southern France, but has many variations. This version is not only pretty to look at, but absolutely delicious to taste. Every time I make a Salade Niçoise and serve it at a party, I wonder why I ever bother with any other starter in the summer.

Cook the potatoes and beans only until they are just done, drain and cool, then chill quickly.

SERVES 4

1 lettuce
250g (8 oz) each small new potatoes and stringless French beans, boiled and cooled
1 bunch of radishes
¼ cucumber, sliced
250g (8 oz) cherry tomatoes, halved
250g (8 oz) can tuna
4 hard-boiled eggs, quartered
12 black olives (optional)
6 anchovy fillets (optional)

FOR THE DRESSING:

120ml (4 fl oz) olive oil
60ml (2 fl oz) lemon juice
1 teaspoon salt
1 teaspoon sugar

Put a layer of the lettuce in a wide pretty bowl, then arrange all the other vegetables in concentric circles on top. Pile the tuna in the centre, adding any oil that it may be packed in but not brine. Arrange the eggs prettily on top. Black olives and thin slices of anchovy complete the authentic Niçoise flavour, although some people find them too intense.

Mix the dressing ingredients thoroughly together, until the sugar and salt have dissolved. Pour over the salad not more than 10 minutes before you serve. Don't toss it, but serve it in sections so that everybody gets a piece of everything. Alternatively, arrange all the vegetables individually in a serving dish and let everyone help themselves.

CRAFTY TIP

A good dressing can make a world of difference to a salad. Always use good ingredients, paying particular attention to the oil. Unrefined oils, for example, olive oil, have a superior flavour – they also cost more! – while those made from various nuts and seeds all have their own special flavour. Always use wine, cider or herb-flavoured vinegar, never malt – it's too harsh. French dressing can be stored in an airtight bottle for several weeks, so it's worth making a lot at a time. Keep in the refrigerator.

Spinach Salad with Mushrooms

One of the great classics of America, a country where salad has moved to the centre of the culinary stage instead of hovering in the wings. Unusual though the ingredients and method are, do try it – you and your guests will be more than pleasantly surprised.

SERVES 4
500g (1 lb) spinach
125g (4 oz) button mushrooms, sliced

FOR THE DRESSING:
225ml (7 fl oz) vegetable oil
125ml (4 fl oz) lemon juice
1 teaspoon clear honey
Pinch of salt

Strip the spinach from its stalks, tear into large bite-size pieces and place in a salad bowl. Add the mushrooms.

Whisk the dressing ingredients together, heat well and pour over the spinach immediately. Toss and serve at once. The hot dressing tenderises the spinach leaves.

Middle Eastern Bread Salad

An unusual combination of ingredients make a very filling yet most refreshing salad. Bread is often used in Middle Eastern cooking in ways which we don't expect – as a basis for meat dishes and, as in this case, the bulk ingredient in a salad. If you can get pitta bread (the flat Greek and Arab style bread) it's much the best for this particular dish. Tahini is a purée of sesame seeds, which is very nutty and rich. It is sold in jars and is now quite widely available.

SERVES 4
4 slices white bread, or pitta bread
*½ cucumber, 8 lettuce leaves, 250g (8 oz) tomatoes, 1 green/red/yellow
    pepper, small bunch of parsley, chopped*
6 each spring onions and radishes, chopped
1 teaspoon tahini (optional)

FOR THE DRESSING:
60ml (2 fl oz) olive oil
3 tablespoons lemon juice
Pinch each of salt and sugar

Dry the bread in the oven until golden, then soak in 2 tablespoons cold water (just enough to make it soggy).

Mix the dressing ingredients together and pour over the prepared vegetables in a salad bowl.

Squeeze the surplus water out of the bread and add to the vegetable mixture with the tahini, if using. Stir and serve.

Salad Elana

The prettiest salad I know and one of the unlikeliest combinations. Do follow the recipe carefully, even to the black pepper over the top at the end. In fact, black pepper eaten with strawberries is very traditional in parts of Britain – it's believed to bring out the flavour. In small quantities, I think it does.

SERVES 4

1 lettuce
1 cucumber, very thinly sliced
500g (1 lb) strawberries, thinly sliced into heart shapes
1 quantity Lemonette Dressing (see page 28)
Freshly ground black pepper

Shred the lettuce into strips like shoe laces and lay as a bed on a china plate. Lay the cucumber in a circle on top and the strawberries on top of that, forming green and red patterns. Pour over the dressing and leave for 1 minute, then sprinkle lightly with black pepper.

Serve with cold poached salmon or with a delicate cold meat, for example, chicken.

Caesar Salad

Despite its Roman name, this is an American salad. The mixture of crisp-fried bread cubes, garlic, Parmesan, lettuce and dressing may seem a little unusual at first, but the combination of textures and the freshness and sharpness of the flavours really works. A great family favourite!

SERVES 4

1 cos lettuce
50g (2 oz) croûtons (see page 36)
Garlic salt
4 tablespoons grated Parmesan cheese

FOR THE DRESSING:

1 egg
125ml (4 fl oz) vegetable oil
3 tablespoons lemon juice
½ tablespoon each salt and sugar

Tear the lettuce into chunks and mix with the croûtons in a bowl.

Put the egg in boiling water for 1 minute, break into a bowl, add the other dressing ingredients and beat until creamy. Pour over the salad and mix it all up. Shake a little garlic salt and the Parmesan cheese over the salad and eat immediately!

Potato Salad

Few vegetables are abused in salad making quite as badly as potatoes. A really good potato salad depends on just three things: the right kind of potatoes; flavouring them while they're still hot; and a properly balanced dressing. The sort of potatoes you need are the kind that don't go floury when they're cooked. Jersey Royals are most commonly available in England but just recently some enterprising supermarkets have been selling the Pink Fir Apple and Kipfler varieties too in season. Any waxy potato, probably yellow-fleshed, is the best kind. Do dress the potatoes while they're still warm – they suck in the flavour in a very special way. Taste the dressing to make sure that it has the right combination of sour, sweet, rich and salty.

SERVES 4
500g (1 lb) potatoes, scrubbed and cut into equal sizes
Pinch of salt
Juice of 1 lemon
4 tablespoons salad oil (olive or groundnut)
1 teaspoon caster sugar
½ teaspoon salt
Freshly ground black pepper
1 tablespoon each chopped parsley and mint

Boil the potatoes from cold with a good pinch of salt. When they're just cooked through but still firm, drain and sprinkle them with half the lemon juice. Mix the rest of the lemon juice with the other dressing ingredients in a jar and give them a good shake, then pour it over the potatoes when they're cool. Don't refrigerate the salad unless you have to. Serve it with cold meat or on its own with good brown bread and butter.

California Gold

This is the kind of salad dish you get in America, specially designed for people who want to believe they're slimming! There this quantity would normally come on a huge plate for one person. I suggest you make it for at least two, especially if you're taking the slimming bit seriously. The flavours are surprisingly well balanced and it does make a light summer lunch on its own.

When this recipe was first broadcast some ten years ago, alfalfa sprouts were very hard to come by in this country, so I suggested mustard and cress. Most healthfood stores now have alfalfa sprouts, which are much thinner than beansprouts and much lighter in texture.

SERVES 2
½ a crisp lettuce
2 carrots, grated
175g (6 oz) alfalfa sprouts (or mustard and cress)
1 avocado, halved and stoned
1 ripe banana
1 egg yolk
150g (5 oz) plain yoghurt
Salt and freshly ground black pepper

Tear the inner leaves of the lettuce into chunks and place on a flattish platter. Mix the carrots and alfalfa sprouts together and pile into the centre of the lettuce. Peel and slice the avocado lengthways. Lay the slices around the outside of the dish. Cut the banana in half, then lengthways into strips and alternate with the avocado.

Beat the egg yolk with the yoghurt and a pinch of salt and pepper to make a golden mayonnaise and pour over the central nest.

CRAFTY TIP

If you want to prepare in advance a salad or starter containing avocado, simply place the avocado stone in the middle of the prepared dish and cover completely with clingfilm. Miraculously – I don't know why! – this stops the avocado discolouring.

The Proof of the Pudding

Crafty puddings aren't that easy to come by and generally fall within three main categories: fruit fools and ice creams can be incredibly crafty, tarts and pies are fairly crafty if you use a processor for the pastry, while fruit-based sweets are simplest of all.

This collection includes perennial favourites of both family and listeners – the Peach Ice Cream once had the biggest number of recipe sheet requests on Capital Radio. I highly recommend it, along with Mango Fool, which is just fantastic, and the Chocolate Mousse. Don't miss the custard recipes, by the way – no one ever pays attention when I broadcast about them but they are the simplest, most nutritious and delicious of all puds and, with the crafty sprinkle, some of the most foolproof.

I've included three basic pastry recipes and a crafty version of Crème Pâtissière at the end of the chapter, all of which are used in the various tarts and pies. You can make the pastries in a food processor or by hand. The processor is just quicker, and I find easier, as pastry is best made as cool and as lightly as possible and I fear I have big, warm hands. However, if you don't want to use the processor technique, mix the pastry on a marble board or in a glass or china bowl using a fork or one of the pastry blenders that are available in kitchen shops these days.

I've included my two favourite apple pie recipes – about as different as you can get (one's a flat flan, the other a deep pie) but both absolutely delicious. I can't choose between them – try them both and see which one you prefer. Both of them, by the way, come virtually unmodified from the earliest days of Capital Radio crafty cooking.

Custard

Real custard (not the gloppy yellow stuff from cans) is a treat and so easy if you use the crafty method – just add the magic sprinkle of cornflour and it doesn't separate or go funny. It was the over-indulgence of cornflour, of course, that led to the packet kind, but hold fast to the faith and try this. You can use it simply as ordinary custard to serve with a pie, in the ice cream or fruit fool recipes that follow or – especially if made with single cream instead of milk – glaze it with caramel to make what the English, not the French, invented, Burnt Custard, or Crème Brûlée as they came to call it across the water.

MAKES 600ML (1 PINT)
600ml (1 pint) creamy milk
1 teaspoon vanilla essence (or 1 vanilla pod)
4 tablespoons caster sugar
1 teaspoon cornflour blended with 1 tablespoon water
2 eggs plus 1 egg yolk

Place the milk and vanilla essence in a pan and heat gently; if using a vanilla pod heat for 20 minutes to let the flavour infuse, then remove pod (you can use it again). Add the sugar to the milk and stir until dissolved, then stir in the blended cornflour. Beat the eggs and egg yolk together and strain into the milk. Heat gently until just simmering, then cook until thickened.

Serve hot with puddings and pies, or leave to cool before using in a recipe.

Crème Brûlée

This is the crafty way to get a crunchy topping to your custard – forget grills and bowls of ice.

SERVES 4
600ml (1 pint) custard (see above, but made with two-thirds milk and
    one-third double cream)
6 tablespoons caster sugar
1 teaspoon water

Leave the custard until it's almost cold, then pour into 4 individual soufflé dishes or ramekins. Place the sugar and water in a heavy-based nonstick saucepan and heat gently, stirring, until the sugar has dissolved, then cook steadily until it turns golden caramel colour. Pour over the custard before it sets and allow to cool. *Don't* chill.

VARIATION

Substitute fruit purée for custard to give, for example, apricot brûlée, strawberry and cream brûlée, or any flavour you fancy.

CRAFTY TIP

When whipping cream for piping, whip only until just stiff – the cream will thicken as it's being piped, from the warmth of the hands on the piping bag.

Crème Caramel

This is the French version of caramel custard – it works well without the caramel too, to make simple custard cups. If you feel nervous about the custard curdling, you can always whip in the crafty teaspoon of cornflour – no one will notice.

SERVES 4
6 tablespoons sugar
1 tablespoon water
600ml (1 pint) milk
2 eggs plus 2 egg yolks
1 teaspoon vanilla essence

Place half the sugar and the water in a heavy-based pan and heat gently, stirring, until the sugar has dissolved, then cook steadily for about 3 minutes, until it caramelises to a light brown. *Don't let it burn.* Pour into a bowl or individual dishes and leave to set.

   Place the milk and remaining sugar in a pan and heat gently, stirring, until the sugar has dissolved. Beat the eggs, egg yolks and vanilla essence together until smooth, then add the milk, still beating. Strain through a sieve into the bowl or dishes and place in a roasting pan containing 2.5cm (1 inch) water. Cook in a preheated oven, 170°C (325°F) gas mark 3, for about 30 minutes or until set. Cool, then unmould onto a serving plate. Serve with single cream and soft fruit.

Fools

I've never worked out why this style of dish is called a fool. It's always seemed dead clever to me. Maybe any fool can do it – this one certainly has for years! The method is always the same: it's the mixtures that can vary with the seasons and the richness or austerity of the rest of the meal.

Although yoghurt is a modern variant, both cream and real custard are classic ingredients for fruit fools. They can be served very rustically or, if you wish, in fine stemmed wine glasses imaginatively decorated for the most elegant of dinner parties.

The mango fool is the most perfect end to a spicy eastern meal I know. As fresh mangoes are hard to come by and not cheap, do use canned purée or liquidise a can of fruit with its syrup – stunning and exotic. Make the variations in the same way as the Apricot Fool – try some of your own ideas, too.

Mango Fool

SERVES 4
300ml (½ pint) double cream
2 tablespoons chopped preserved ginger
2 tablespoons ginger syrup
500g (1 lb) can mango purée or 1 can mangoes, crushed

Whip the cream until thick but not grainy. Stir in the ginger and syrup, then the mango purée. Fold carefully so as to keep bulky. Chill. Serve with thin sweet biscuits – *tuiles* or *langues de chat* are nice.

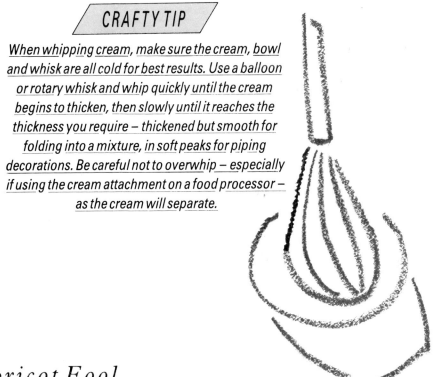

Apricot Fool

SERVES 4

500g (1 lb) fresh apricots, or 1 can apricots
300ml (¹/₂ pint) double cream
50g (2 oz) slivered almonds

If using fresh apricots, cook with 175g (6 oz) sugar in 175ml (6 fl oz) water for 15 minutes, until tender. Skin and stone. Purée the apricots with the cooking liquid, or the canned apricots with their juice, in a food processor or blender until smooth. Whip the cream until really thick, then stir in half the almonds. Mix the purée and cream together, spoon into individual dishes and chill for about 2 hours, until set. Sprinkle the remaining almonds on top to serve.

VARIATIONS

Gooseberry purée and custard, or custard plus yoghurt: serve with ginger biscuits.
Blackcurrant purée with cream and yoghurt.
Strawberry purée and cream, with whole strawberries mixed in.
Plum purée with cream and custard: damsons are best, well sweetened.

Ice Cream

The technique for all crafty ice creams is the same. You don't need a machine and you don't get ice crystals. You don't need to beat it halfway through the freezing time, either. The proper name for this method is a *parfait*, though I discovered it in a Lavender Hill Chinese take-away years ago and have been using it ever since.

When we had to think of new things to do with strawberries and cream for a recent television programme, we made this ice cream with them and it was an outright winner. Not that it's new really – just an old crafty technique brought up to date.

You can, by the way, substitute a limited amount of plain yoghurt or real custard for the cream, but the more you add (unless you beat it or have a special ice cream machine) the more ice crystal crunchy it gets – the price you pay for healthy eating, I suppose, though the flavour doesn't suffer much. Anyway, try the original recipe first and decide for yourself.

Peach Ice Cream

SERVES 4

150ml (¼ pint) water
125g (4 oz) caster sugar
2 peaches, skinned and thinly sliced
3 eggs (at room temperature)
50g (2 oz) icing sugar, sifted
1 teaspoon vanilla essence
150ml (¼ pint) whipping cream

Place the water and caster sugar in a pan and heat gently, stirring, until the sugar has dissolved and a syrup formed. Add the peaches and cook for 5 minutes, then cool.

Whisk the eggs and icing sugar together in a warm bowl until double their volume. Add the vanilla essence.

Whip the cream with 2 tablespoons of the peach syrup in a separate bowl until thick but not stiff.

Remove the peaches from the syrup and cut into small pieces. Mix the fruit, egg mixture and cream together quickly and lightly. (You don't use the rest of the peach syrup). Cover, seal and freeze for at least 2 hours. If rock hard, allow to soften in the fridge for 1 hour before serving.

VARIATIONS

Vanilla Ice Cream: just leave out the peaches.
Strawberry or any other fruit: leave out the vanilla essence and peaches and add 150ml (¼ pint) fruit purée or thick fruit juices.
Coffee or chocolate: leave out the fruit and vanilla and add ½ cup *strong* coffee or cocoa to the egg mixture before mixing in the cream.

CRAFTY TIP

No need to top and tail soft fruits like blackcurrants, gooseberries, if you're going to purée them. Simply rub the cooked fruit through a fine sieve or mouli and all the bits get left behind. It's slower than using a food processor or blender, but still quicker and easier than the initial chore!

Marmalade Ice Cream

An unexpected version but very good, especially in the winter when soft fruit is scarce.

SERVES 4

3 eggs, separated
75g (3 oz) icing sugar, sifted
150ml (¼ pint) double cream
4 tablespoons marmalade with peel

Beat the egg yolks with the icing sugar until creamy. Whisk the egg whites until stiff. Beat the cream until thick but *not* stiff. Mix the marmalade into the egg yolk mixture, add the cream, then the egg whites. Mix gently, then pour into a container, cover, seal and freeze for at least 6 hours.

Soften in the fridge for 1 hour before serving with shortcake biscuits.

Blackberry Cobbler

This is a simple country-style pudding for the autumn and winter. In my family it's known as DHP, or Darned Hot Pudding, as it takes quite a while to cool to eating temperature. It's beautiful to look at, with a golden top stained purple at the edges with the fragrant fruit. This, unchanged, is one of the earliest of all the crafty cooking recipes.

CRAFTY TIP

If you want to cut down on your cream intake, replace half the quantity of cream with yoghurt. To use in puddings or for decoration, whip double cream first until fairly thick, then add the yoghurt and whip again until thick. For a pouring accompaniment, simply stir single cream and yoghurt together.

SERVES 4

500g (1 lb) blackberries
125g (4 oz) sugar

FOR THE TOPPING:

125g (4 oz) self-raising flour, sifted
125g (4 oz) sugar
25g (1 oz) butter, melted (or 1 tablespoon oil)
1 egg, beaten
200ml (⅓ pint) milk

Whisk all the topping ingredients together to form a batter the consistency of double cream. Mix the blackberries and sugar together and place in a deep pie dish or casserole. Cover with the batter, smooth the top and bake in a preheated oven, 190°C (375°F) gas mark 5, for 25–30 minutes, until brown and risen. It will crack at the top and the juice will show through, but don't worry, it's meant to.

Chocolate Mousse

This is the magic mousse mixture. Don't worry about it and don't be tempted to change the quantities. I once experimented for a whole day to improve on the original and failed. The more bitter the chocolate, the better the taste – and unsalted butter is best – otherwise, *bon appetit!*

SERVES 4
125g (4 oz) plain dark chocolate
4 tablespoons high juice orange squash
50g (2 oz) unsalted butter
4 eggs, separated

Place the chocolate and squash in a pan and heat very gently until melted, stirring frequently. Beat in the butter, then remove from the heat and beat in the egg yolks, one at a time. Leave to cool.

Whisk the egg whites until *really* stiff. Fold into the chocolate mixture and pour into pretty cups. Chill for at least 2 hours. Serve with crisp, nutty biscuits.

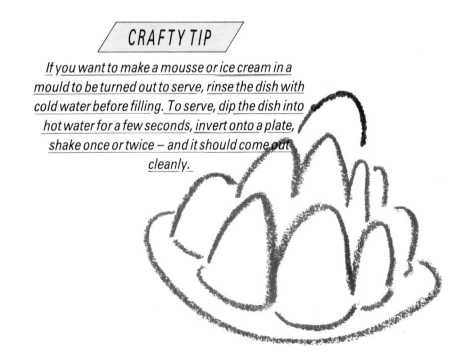

CRAFTY TIP

If you want to make a mousse or ice cream in a mould to be turned out to serve, rinse the dish with cold water before filling. To serve, dip the dish into hot water for a few seconds, invert onto a plate, shake once or twice – and it should come out cleanly.

Apple Pancakes

Called Jacques in France where I first found them. These are really simple and can be made ad infinitum, which is a useful factor when you see how quickly they can be eaten.

SERVES 4
125g (4 oz) plain flour, sifted
50g (2 oz) caster sugar
1 egg, beaten
1 tablespoon vegetable oil
Pinch of salt
225ml (7 fl oz) orange juice
1 large cooking apple, cored and grated

Mix the flour, sugar, egg, oil and salt together. Beat in the orange juice to make a thick cream, then add the apple. Drop tablespoons of the mixture into a heavy-based frying pan brushed with oil. (You can get 2 or 3 into the pan at a time.) Cook for 2–3 minutes, until browned, then brown the other side.

Sandwich together in pairs with butter, apple jelly, apricot jam or honey and serve hot with thick cream.

Baked Apples

The simplest of dishes, transformed by using large eating apples and adding a little liquid to the baking dish.

SERVES 4
4 large eating apples (for example, Russets, Cox's)
4 tablespoons mixed dried fruit
4 teaspoons golden syrup, honey, marmalade or any jam
4 teaspoons butter

Core the apples almost to the bottom, making a 'well'. Draw a sharp knife round the equator of the fruit, just cutting the skin – this stops splitting. Fill each 'well' with 1 tablespoon dried fruit, top each with 1 teaspoon syrup, honey, marmalade or jam, and dot the top with the butter. Place in a baking dish containing 1–2.5cm (½–1 inch) water (depending how much juice you want) and bake in a preheated oven, 180°C (350°F) gas mark 4, for 30 minutes.

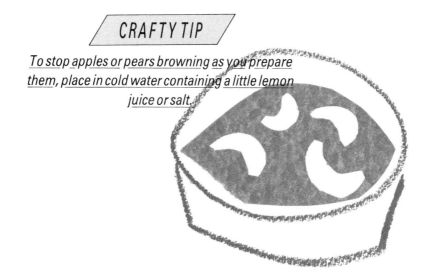

CRAFTY TIP

To stop apples or pears browning as you prepare them, place in cold water containing a little lemon juice or salt.

Fruit Surprise

An early crafty recipe from a 'Dishes of the World' series I broadcast in the early 1970s. It's known in France as a clafoutis and cherries or apples are the usual fruit. The surprise is you can use almost any fruit (except berries) and it works really well. Slice large fruits, use soft or small fruits whole, removing any stones or pips.

SERVES 4

2 eggs, beaten
175g (6 oz) plain flour, sifted
75g (3 oz) caster sugar
Pinch of salt
25g (1 oz) butter, melted
200ml (⅓ pint) milk
½ tablespoon vanilla essence
500g (1 lb) prepared fruit – apples, cherries, raspberries and plums are
    best
50g (2 oz) soft brown sugar

Beat together the eggs, flour, caster sugar, salt and butter until smooth. Add the milk and beat to form a thick batter, then stir in the vanilla essence. Pour into a buttered flan dish or flat china dish. Mix the fruit with the brown sugar and tip evenly into the batter. Bake in a preheated oven, 180°C (350°F) gas mark 4, for 45 minutes or until well browned. Serve it from the dish with lots of pouring cream.

American Apple Pie

A deep dish pie this, with a very different flavour and texture when it's cooked. It's very often eaten in America hot out of the oven, with a large dollop of vanilla ice cream, and is known as pie-à-la-mode. Even if you eat it cold, it's still very nice with thick cream or ice cream ladled on top of it.

SERVES 6–8

750g (1½ lb) eating apples, peeled, cored and quartered
1 tablespoon cornflour
1 tablespoon lemon juice
1 quantity Shortcrust Pastry (see page 200)
175g (6 oz) caster sugar
1 teaspoon each ground cinnamon and cloves
25g (1 oz) butter
Beaten egg or milk to glaze

Place the apples, cornflour and lemon juice in the processor bowl and process briefly until the apples are chopped but still in chunks, and the cornflour and lemon juice have been mixed all over them.

Line a 20 cm (8 inch) pie dish, 3.5cm (1½ inches) deep, with half the pastry, pile in the apple mixture and sprinkle with the sugar and spices. Make sure the middle's piled at least 2.5 cm (1 inch) higher than the edge of the dish to prevent the pie sinking in the middle when it's cooked. Dot the surface of the apples with the butter and cover with the remaining pastry, wetting the rim first to make sure it will stick. Brush the top with a little beaten egg or milk, cut two slits in the centre and bake in a preheated oven, 200°C (400°F) gas mark 6, for 40 minutes. Turn off the heat and let the pie cook for another 5 minutes in the switched-off oven.

If serving cold, let it cool all the way down in the oven.

CRAFTY TIP

Cook dried fruits in their soaking water, to retain their full flavour and nutrients. Try soaking them in tea as an alternative.

French Apple Flan

The Gallic way with apples – as far away from the American as it's possible to get and still make an apple tart, it is equally delicious – 'Vive la différence'.

SERVES 8

1 quantity Pâte Sablée (see page 199)
600ml (1 pint) Crème Pâtissière (see page 201)
6 eating apples, cored (and peeled if you prefer)
4 tablespoons caster sugar
4 tablespoons apricot jam, melted

Roll out the pastry and use to line an oblong tin about 36×20cm (14×8 inches) – a Swiss roll tin is ideal. Prick all over, line with foil, weigh down with dried beans or rice, and 'bake blind' in a preheated oven, 200°C (400°F) gas mark 6, for 15–20 minutes. Leave to cool, then spread with the cooled crème pâtissière.

Divide each apple into 12 pieces, like orange segments, and lay in overlapping rows on the crème. Sprinkle with the sugar and glaze under a *hot* grill for 3 minutes; don't let the edges of the pastry burn – make sure by covering carefully with the apples, or foil. Pour over the apricot jam to glaze and leave to cool. Don't refrigerate unless you have to.

Apricot Tart

Along with the classic French Apple Flan, apricot tart is the other absolute *le must* as the chic French phrase has it. There is scarcely a restaurant from three-star-Michelin to transport-café-Routier that would regard itself as properly equipped to serve lunch or dinner without an apricot tart to hand.

One of the nice things about this tart is that it can be made any time of the year – not only during the brief fortnight when the fresh scented golden balls arrive for their too short a season – as you get delicious results with well chosen canned apricots.

SERVES 6

1 quantity Pâte Sablée (see page 199)
300ml (½ pint) Crème Pâtissière (see page 201)
500g (1 lb) can apricot halves or 500g (1 lb) fresh apricots
1 dessertspoon arrowroot

Grease a 20cm (8 inch) flan tin (or use a nonstick one). Roll out the pastry and use to line the tin, or knuckle it out carefully to the shape of the tin. Line with foil and weigh down with dried beans or rice and 'bake blind' in a preheated oven, 200°C (400°F) gas mark 6, for 15 minutes. Remove the foil and beans and return the shell to the oven for 10–15 minutes, until a golden biscuit colour. (It's not going to go into the oven again and needs to be thoroughly cooked at this stage.) Leave to cool, then fill with the crème pâtissière to within about 1cm (½ inch) from the top.

Drain the canned apricots (if using), reserving the syrup, or cook the fresh ones with 175g (6 oz) sugar in 175ml (6 fl oz) water for about 15 minutes, until tender. Remove the skins, stone and halve. Place the apricots, cut side down, in neat patterns on the crème pâtissière.

Add the arrowroot to half the syrup, bring to the boil, stirring, then simmer for 1 minute. Leave to cool a little, then pour over the apricots, filling the gaps between them and making sure that it doesn't overflow the edges of the tart. Leave to set and, if you like, chill for about 1 hour before serving. The juice will form a lovely clear coating for the apricots through which a little of the crème pâtissière will show as a golden glow.

VARIATIONS

Peach Tart

Use peaches or nectarines in exactly the same way. Fresh ones are best and best of all are the white peaches that you can sometimes buy – I think most of them come from China. They have the added advantage of not being too large and so fit the shape and design of the flan tin rather well. If you use canned peaches, try not to buy the sliced ones as they somehow look more synthetic than halves do.

Cherry Tart

You can make cherry tart in a similar way, using those lovely dark juicy cherries that are with us for such a short time in the summer. In an ideal world, of course, you'd take the stones out first, but I find that life is too short and anyone who doesn't have the patience to spit out a few stones for the sake of the incredible flavour of fresh cherries isn't worth the trouble!

You can, if you like, pre-cook the cherries for just 5 minutes in a little sugar and water to soften them, if they're not totally ripe. Use 175g (6 oz) bramble jelly heated with 2 tablespoons lemon juice for the glaze (omit the arrowroot).

Strawberry and Cherry Tarts

MAKES ABOUT 12

A mixture of individual strawberry and cherry tarts makes one of the most incredible and irresistible teatime treats I know. Make 5cm (2 inch) pastry cases and 'bake blind' as on page 193 for just 10 minutes. Put 1 tablespoon of lightly whipped cream in each, then fill with strawberries or cherries. Use 4 tablespoons redcurrant jelly heated with 2 tablespoons water for the glaze (omit the arrowroot). Serve within 4 hours.

Custard Tart

Old English custard tart is the sort of pastry you used to see in bakers' shops in the days when they made their bread and cakes themselves. There are fewer who bake like that these days, but the combination of creamy custard with its nutmeg flavouring and crumbly pastry brings back for me childhood memories associated with some of the best things to eat. It's also a very simple tart that keeps well for two or three days in the fridge, if covered with foil or clingfilm.

SERVES 6

½ quantity Pâte Sablée (see page 199)
2 eggs plus 1 yolk
5 tablespoons milk
4 tablespoons caster sugar
1 teaspoon ground nutmeg (or grated fresh)

Line a 20cm (8 inch) pie dish or tart tin with the pastry, making a neat fluted edge at the top with the back of a fork. Whisk the eggs, egg yolk, milk and sugar together until thoroughly mixed, then strain through a sieve into the pastry case. Sprinkle the nutmeg on top and bake in a preheated oven, 220°C (425°F) gas mark 7, for 35 minutes. Check after 25 minutes to make sure the pastry isn't burning or the top of the custard cooking too quickly. Try to avoid opening the oven door more than you have to so that the custard gets a chance to set. Switch off the heat and let the tart cool in the oven for 5–6 minutes, then place in a draught-free place until cold and set.

Perfect Pastry

You can make pastry by hand or in a food processor – I prefer the processor. It is a good idea to chill the pastry for about 30 minutes in the refrigerator before you use it. It really does make a difference.

Pâte Brisée

Pâte brisée is the French answer to savoury pastry. It's usually made as a base for the many different types of quiches and open pies that the French adore as first courses, or as a main course for a light meal. It's a rather tougher material than our shortcrust pastry and can be handled more firmly and shaped more thinly. The key to this extra strength is the egg yolk, which goes into the pastry. Don't be tempted to leave it out. The quantities given are for one 20–25cm (8–10 inch) open flan. This recipe uses the processor – you can make it by hand.

150g (5 oz) plain flour
½ teaspoon salt
50g (2 oz) butter, roughly chopped
1 egg yolk
1½–2 tablespoons cold water

Place the flour, salt and butter in the processor bowl and process for about 5 seconds, until the mixture resembles very coarse breadcrumbs. With the motor running, add the egg yolk and water through the feed tube and process until the mixture starts to ball up around the knife. Stop the machine running and tip the dough out on to a floured board. Knead it two or three times with the heel of your hand so that it forms a solid coherent mass, wrap it in foil or clingfilm and chill for at least 30 minutes – up to a couple of hours won't hurt.

When you're ready to use it, you can either roll it out on a floured board in the normal manner or press it into the tin with the knuckles of your hand, which is my favourite method.

Pâte Sablée

This sweet shortcrust pastry (the French version of our own shortcrust) is called *sablée* (which means sand) because it is so crisp and sugary that when eaten it just crumbles away like a sandcastle in front of the tide. It's not all that dry or gritty, just incredibly soft textured, but surprisingly strong and firm, carrying the fruits and cream fillings that the French are so fond of. Unlike our own shortcrust it is also very useful for filling with raw ingredients, as the addition of the egg gives the pastry a surprising degree of water resistance and strength.

This pastry is so delicious that in parts of France they don't use it as a case at all, but roll it out flat, cut it with biscuit cutters and make what are called *sablées* – buttery biscuits. Sometimes they cover them with slivered almonds before they're baked. If you have any pastry left over, it's certainly worth trying this.

MAKES 125G (4 OZ)
125g (4 oz) plain flour, sifted
1½ tablespoons caster sugar
50g (2 oz) butter, diced
Pinch of salt
1 egg

Place the flour, sugar, butter and salt in the processor bowl and process for 5–10 seconds, until it resembles fine breadcrumbs. With the motor running, pour in the egg through the feed tube. Stop the machine the moment the dough starts to form a ball. Tip it onto a floured board, press it all together with the heel of your hand, squash it flat a couple of times, kneading it lightly, then finally roll it up into a ball. Wrap in clingfilm and chill for at least 30 minutes. (It won't suffer if it's kept tightly wrapped in the fridge for up to 3 days.) Use as required.

Shortcrust Pastry

If you have a favourite shortcrust pastry recipe, try making it in the processor, rubbing the flour and fat together first and adding the liquid afterwards. My own experience in this is that any recipe I'm used to making by hand probably needs a little more flour added to it when using a processor, as the blending and mixing is rather more thorough than you can achieve by hand. Don't add much water, but add it bit by bit as the pastry will suddenly ball up around the blade. If you don't have a favourite shortcrust recipe, try using this one.

It's interesting to note here that, despite the enormous change in people's tastes in recent years, from white towards wholemeal brown bread, the same hasn't been true in pastry making and, committed though I am to healthy eating, I have to say that I've never really met with top-class pastry made with anything but white flour.

MAKES 175G (6 OZ)
175g (6 oz) plain flour
50g (2 oz) butter, cut into 2–3 pieces
Pinch of salt
2–3 tablespoons water

Place the flour, butter and salt in the processor bowl and process for 5–10 seconds, until the mixture resembles fairly coarse breadcrumbs. (You may need to scrape the side of the bowl down once during the process.) With the motor running, add the water 1 tablespoon at a time through the feed tube. Flours vary as to the amount of water they can absorb, so you'll have to check as you go. Stop the machine as soon as the pastry forms a ball around the blade. Scrape out the bowl thoroughly and very gently press all the pastry pieces together into one solid lump. Wrap in foil or clingfilm and chill for about 30 minutes. Use as required.

Treacle Tart

This rich, rib-sticking, Old English tart is made with ingredients easily found, yet it always seems special. If you don't want to use walnuts, the same quantity of toasted breadcrumbs make a traditional substitute, while hazelnuts are more than an acceptable alternative. Grated apple is sometimes suggested as a possible addition but never seems to work too well with me, because the juice from the apple makes the treacle itself go soggy.

SERVES 6 GENEROUSLY
175g (6 oz) golden syrup
2 eggs, beaten
Juice of 1 lemon
50g (2 oz) walnuts, finely chopped (or dry toasted breadcrumbs)
½ quantity Pâte Sablée (see page 199)

Mix the syrup, eggs and lemon juice together in a warm bowl until thoroughly blended. (A warm bowl prevents the treacle sticking to the side.) Stir in the walnuts.

Line a 20cm (8 inch) tart tin with the pastry, reserving the trimmings. Pour in the treacle, making sure it doesn't overflow the pastry as it will rise when it cooks. Use the trimmings to make a lattice pattern over the filling. Bake in a preheated oven, 200°C (400°F) gas mark 6, for 35 minutes, or until the filling is golden brown and risen.

Serve warm or cold.

Crème Pâtissière

The most sumptuous part of French *tartes* for most foreigners is the fact that just beneath the fruit and before you get to the crisp pastry, there is a layer of what tastes like vanilla-flavoured cream. It's called *crème pâtissière* or bakers' cream and although it was originally developed as a substitute for the more expensive real stuff, I often actually prefer it. It is one of the easiest things in the world to make and transforms an ordinary tart into something else! With a processor, of course, a lot of the art is already taken care of for you, so you can earn the plaudits without having to struggle.

MAKES 600ML (1 PINT)
75g (3 oz) caster sugar
2 eggs

50g (2 oz) plain flour
450ml (¾ pint) milk
½ teaspoon vanilla essence

Place the sugar and eggs in the processor bowl and process until really smoothly blended together. Add the flour and process until smoothly mixed. Bring the milk to the boil then, with the motor running, pour it carefully through the feed tube into the bowl. Process for a further 5 seconds. Return to the saucepan and cook over a low heat for 5 minutes, stirring, until the mixture thickens completely and the flour is all cooked. Add the vanilla essence and leave to cool, stirring it occasionally to prevent a skin forming. Use as required. It will keep in the fridge for up to a week if it's covered.

Crafty Cakes and Beautiful Baking

Cake making and bread baking are things that have come to crafty cooking comparatively late in life. It's not that I don't enjoy baking, although I have never been convinced about its position where so many home economics courses place it, in the heartland of cooking. It's more that producing really crafty cakes depends on two technical developments that have become widespread only in the last ten years: soft margarine, and then food processors. Both helped, but together they were a revelation. Soft margarine, you see, made the 'all in one' method of making a cake mixture really easy, and the food processor meant that you could do it all in the sealed bowl in about twenty seconds. What could be craftier? Not even a cake mix as I discovered when one of the leading cookery demonstrators, using the most popular mix on sale, and I, using the recipe you will find on page 202, had a light-hearted competition to test speed and flavour in mixing and cooking. The Crafty Chocolate Cake was mixed and baking in time to allow me to open the oven for its rival to be put in. It also won hands down in the taste test, although, of course, both cakes took the same length of time to bake. That's one of the cardinal rules of crafty baking: nothing will shorten time in the oven (or fridge . . . see the yummy Belgian Chocolate Cake) but that's not time you have to spend waiting, or even watching if you have a timer with a loud ping! The crafty techniques are all in the mixing and preparation.

The same is true for bread. I have given a number of recipes for various kinds of bread, and while one of the crafty techniques at least offers an almost miraculous shortening of the whole process, none saves time in the oven. Bread has always been an object of reverence throughout history, with many religions and cultures (including Christianity) attaching a ritual importance to it. It's not then too surprising that the staff of life should in many ways be the touchstone of the change in our eating habits. The Campaign for Real Bread, with or without capital letters in its title, has been the most successful of all the consumer battles to improve the quality of our food. And what a success! Big 'plant' bakeries closing, and flourishing small bakers newly emerging from the doldrums. Even supermarkets now relegate the plastic wrapper to a side aisle, while the 'in store' fresh bread bakery takes pride of place (and smell) in the centre of the shop. Fifteen years ago, as a nation, we ate an insignificant amount of brown bread and most of that was one of a few branded varieties. Since the wholemeal revolution all has changed – nearly a third of the bread we buy now is whole grain or 'brown', or is fibre enriched, and that proportion is increasing every year. We have taken to the flavour, texture and healthy properties of real bread in a big way; you could say it's selling like hot cakes, only these days it's the hot bread shops doing the selling.

Why then make it at home? Many think it's a long and difficult process, not worth the bother. It's true the bread may take its time, but it's not your time, and these days combination ovens with microwaves can cut down baking times (follow the instructions for your own model for best results). And as for difficult, there are few cooking processes easier to manage, or more satisfying. Except for the fortunate few who can devote themselves to constant pleasure, bread making is not, however, a daily occurrence. Indeed, in my experience, the occasions when people most want to be reminded of recipes are in times of crisis. I can remember vividly the big bakery strike (many think it began the revival of real bread), in the early years of crafty cooking on Capital Radio, and the demand for bread recipes and techniques that ensued. More recently, when the great blizzard of 1987 immobilised most of south-east England, on local radio again, Kent's Invicta, it was the bread recipes that communities and people cut off for days both wanted and needed.

The great thing about bread is to treat it with respect but not fear. The processes that make dough rise, the crust go brown, and that delicious smell fill the house, are very robust. You really have to make a terrible set of mistakes to make terrible bread. Using the simple and traditional methods with fresh or dried yeast, the whole process should take about three hours. But only about twenty-five minutes of that is going to be *your* time, in three little bursts at hourly intervals. The rest is occupied by the wonderful chemical and biological processes that look after themselves. If you use the crafty baking accelerator, or one of the soda bread recipes, the time will be cut by nearly two hours. But even then most of the remaining period will be spent with the bread in the oven, and the crafty cooks with their feet up.

Chocolate Cake

This is the ultimate crafty cake – chocolate, yummy and effortless. It produces a dark, rich, moist cake that, if you can bear it, keeps well. It's the recipe we tested on television against the WI's top cake mix variety. It was the winner on taste and took half the time to make (though just as long to bake).

MAKES ONE 20CM (8 INCH) CAKE
175g (6 oz) plain flour
5 tablespoons caster sugar
3 tablespoons cocoa powder (not drinking chocolate)
1 teaspoon baking powder
2 eggs
150ml (¼ pint) each cooking oil and milk
1 tablespoon black treacle

Place all the dry ingredients in a bowl and stir to mix. Beat all the other ingredients together in a jug, then add to the dry mix. Stir with a wooden spoon for about 1½ minutes, until thoroughly blended.

Transfer the mixture to two greased 20cm (8 inch) sponge tins or a 20cm (8 inch) cake tin and bake in a preheated oven, 190°C (375°F) gas mark 5: two tins take 25–30 minutes, 1 tin takes 45–50 minutes. The top should spring back when lightly pressed if done. Cool on a wire rack.

Decorate with melted chocolate or icing sugar sprinkled through a cut-out stencil. Apricot jam is the traditional filling.

Belgian Chocolate Cake

I don't know where the crafty Belgian is who first had this idea, but I hope he's rich and happy! A dead simple confection that is a great favourite with children – to make as well as eat. Cut it in small slices, you'll be amazed how filling it is.

MAKES ONE 20 CM (8 INCH) CAKE
250g (8 oz) biscuits (sweet or mixed savoury and sweet)
125g (4 oz) butter or margarine
125g (4 oz) golden syrup
125g (4 oz) cocoa powder
50–125g (2–4 oz) chopped nuts or raisins (or a mixture)
Grated rind of 1 orange

Crush the biscuits roughly, place in a pan with the other ingredients and heat until the mixture has melted and mixed together. Turn into a 20cm (8 inch) flat dish (a quiche tin is fine) lined with foil and flatten firmly with the back of a spoon. Place in the refrigerator for at least 2 hours, until set.

A final touch if you like: melt about 50g (2 oz) plain chocolate with 2 tablespoons orange juice and pour over the top of the cake before you put it in the fridge.

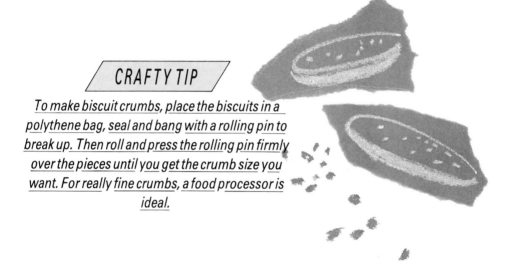

CRAFTY TIP

To make biscuit crumbs, place the biscuits in a polythene bag, seal and bang with a rolling pin to break up. Then roll and press the rolling pin firmly over the pieces until you get the crumb size you want. For really fine crumbs, a food processor is ideal.

Little Scarlet Sponge

This is a crafty version of the Victoria sponge – it's virtually foolproof and can be flavoured with orange, lemon or coffee to create variety. A food processor helps with this – if you use one put all the ingredients except the jam in at once and process for 15 seconds.

MAKES ONE 20CM (8 INCH) CAKE
125g (4 oz) butter or margarine
125g (4 oz) caster sugar
2 eggs
125g (4 oz) self-raising wheatmeal or white flour
1 heaped teaspoon baking powder
175g (6 oz) strawberry jam

Beat the fat and sugar together until creamy, then beat in the eggs. Sift in the flour and baking powder and mix until smooth. Pour into a 20cm (8 inch) nonstick, or greased, cake tin and bake in a preheated oven, 190°C (375°F) gas mark 5, for 25 minutes, until the cake is springy to touch. Cool, then remove from the tin.

Split in half horizontally and sandwich with the jam. If you like, decorate it with patterns of icing sugar. I have been known to fill the centre with cream as well when no one is looking. Not crafty, but mmmmmm . . . !

Strawberry Shortcake

Although strawberry shortcake has always seemed to me an American invention, this version came from Denmark where the unsalted butter that makes it so delicious is also produced. It makes wonderful biscuits, too, treated slightly differently as I've indicated below.

MAKES ONE 18CM (7 INCH) CAKE
175g (6 oz) unsalted butter (or margarine)
250g (10 oz) self-raising flour, sifted
75g (3 oz) caster sugar

FOR THE FILLING AND TOPPING:
250g (8 oz) strawberries
150ml (5 fl oz) double cream (or half cream and yoghurt), whipped

Make sure that the butter or margarine is soft (not the softened variety of margarine, though – and don't make them liquid by melting them). Mix with the flour and sugar to a stiff dough. Press into an 18cm (7 inch) cake tin, level the top, then prick all over with a fork.

Bake in a preheated oven, 200°C (400°F) gas mark 6, for 20 minutes, keeping an eye on it. If the top starts to brown too soon, cover it with a piece of buttered paper.

Turn it out onto a wire rack and, whilst still warm but not hot, split in half horizontally. Leave to cool, then sandwich together with half the strawberries and cream. Repeat on top of the cake, decorating it with the best whole fruit.

VARIATION

Press the mixture into a Swiss roll tin, divide into 5cm (2 inch) oblongs and decorate with pieces of almond or cherries. Bake for 15 minutes only and you have really delicious shortbread.

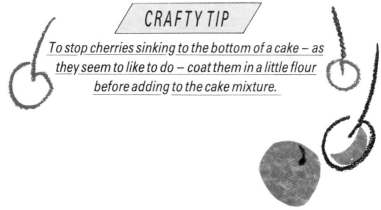

CRAFTY TIP

To stop cherries sinking to the bottom of a cake – as they seem to like to do – coat them in a little flour before adding to the cake mixture.

Christmas Cake

This is the original 'one bowl mix' crafty Christmas cake. There have been others since – low fat and high fibre versions especially for recent television programmes – but I'm always meeting people who began making this lovely cake nearly fifteen years ago when it was first broadcast and have made it every year since. It may be the most popular crafty recipe ever, for every Christmas the demand for the recipe is unfailing. Here it is again – Merry Christmas, or whenever you make it.

MAKES ONE 25CM (10 INCH) CAKE

350g (12 oz) self-raising flour, sifted
350g (12 oz) soft brown sugar (not demerara)
350g (12 oz) butter or margarine (left at room temperature for 30 minutes)
125g (4 oz) ground almonds
6 eggs
1 dessertspoon baking powder
½ teaspoon salt
6 tablespoons milk
125g (4 oz) each glacé cherries and cut peel
350g (12 oz) each raisins, sultanas and currants

Place the flour, sugar, butter or margarine, ground almonds, eggs, baking powder and salt in a large bowl, mix well, then beat until smooth. Add the milk – the spoon should leave a trail which doesn't vanish immediately. Add all the fruit and mix well. Put the mixture into a large greased 25cm (10 inch) round cake tin lined with greaseproof paper and bake in a preheated oven, 180°C (350°F) gas mark 4, for 2½ hours. Check after 1½ hours: if the top is brown, cover with greaseproof paper.

To check if it's done, place a skewer in the middle: if it comes out clean it's cooked, if it comes out with batter on it, it needs another 15–20 minutes. Leave to cool in the tin for 20 minutes, then turn out onto a wire rack to cool thoroughly.

You can marzipan and ice it; eat as it is (my favourite); or before baking decorate the top with whole almonds for a Dundee cake.

Bread

All wheat is milled one of two ways: either in old-fashioned stone mills which grind all the wheat up together at once, or in roller mills (invented in the last century) which take out the coarser brown parts of the flour before grinding down the very fine white sections. White flour is ground from 70 per cent of the grain, wholemeal from 100 per cent and the variations between, usually known as wheatmeal, range between 80 and 87 per cent.

The enriched flours like VitBe, Hovis and Granary have some of the bran and wheatgerm that has been extracted in the roller milling process added back into them.

Some experts believe that this method produces bread which has a better rise to it than the slower milled and never quite so fine stoneground wheatmeal. The stoneground supporters, on the other hand, believe that the roller milling destroys some of the nutrition and the nutty flavour of the wholewheat. It's really all a matter of personal taste.

HINT 1

If you can't find fresh yeast from a local baker's or health food store for your home baking, use dried yeast or one of the new instant dried yeasts that don't need pre-mixing. Read the instructions carefully and don't use too much: more yeast won't give a better rise to your bread, it'll merely make it drier and possibly cause it to crack open while baking.

HINT 2

To test when loaves are done, rap the base with your knuckle – the loaf should sound hollow. If you bake it for the time given and it doesn't sound like that, tip it out of the tin and leave it on its side in the oven for another 5 minutes or so, after which it should be fine.

HINT 3

Always cool bread on a wire rack and don't eat it too hot. Delicious though it may seem, it's very indigestible until it's cooled to room temperature. Most bread improves by being left for at least 12 hours after it's cooked to mature and settle. It also slices a lot better then, too.

Wholemeal Bread

MAKES 2 LARGE OR 3 SMALL LOAVES
25g (1 oz) fresh yeast, or 1 packet dried
15g (½ oz) soft brown sugar
600ml (1 pint) warm water
1kg (2 lb) wholemeal flour
1 teaspoon salt
1 tablespoon sunflower or soya oil

Blend the yeast, sugar and 1 cup of the water together and leave to froth. Mix the flour, salt and oil together in a large bowl. Add the yeast mixture and remaining water and knead until elastic and smooth. Cover and leave in a warm place for 1 hour to rise. Knead again, then put into 2 large or 3 small greased tins and leave until the dough reaches the top of the tins. Bake in a preheated oven, 220°C (425°F) gas mark 7, for 45–55 minutes, then test (see Hint 2). Transfer to a wire rack and allow to cool.

VARIATIONS

Wholemeal Fruit Loaf

When kneading for the second time, add 50g (2 oz) butter, 175g (6 oz) mixed dried fruit and 1 teaspoon mixed spice.

Granary Bread

Add 1 tablespoon malt extract or molasses to the basic ingredients. Replace half the wholemeal flour with granary flour.

White Bread

'Strong' unbleached white flour has the best rising properties of all for making bread. It makes a creamy coloured loaf with a lovely textured crumb.

MAKES 2 LARGE LOAVES
25g (1 oz) fresh yeast plus 15g (½ oz) white sugar or 1 tablespoon dried
 yeast with a pinch of sugar
600ml (1 pint) warm water
1kg (2 lb) unbleached white flour
1 teaspoon salt
1 teaspoon salad oil

Cream the yeast with a little of the warm water and the sugar until it's frothy. Mix with the other ingredients and knead thoroughly. Cover and leave in a warm place for 1½ hours to rise. Knead again, then put into 2 large greased tins and leave until the dough reaches the top of the tins. Bake in a preheated oven, 220°C (425°F) gas mark 7, for 45–50 minutes, then test (see Hint 2). Cool on a wire rack.

VARIATIONS

Cheese and Herb Loaf

Add 125g (4 oz) grated cheese and 1 tablespoon each chopped parsley and spring onion when kneading the second time. Sprinkle more grated cheese on the top just before baking for a tangy flavour.

Bread Rolls

Use the same mixtures as for any of the breads. On the second kneading, divide the dough up into 50–125g (2–4 oz) balls. Give each one a roll on a flat surface with your hand until it's oval. Leave to rise for 20 minutes. Sprinkle with flour, or egg, and seed them with cracked wheat or sesame seeds. Bake as for bread but only 15–20 minutes.

Pizza

On the second kneading, add 7 teaspoons olive oil and roll out into two 30cm (12 inch) rounds 1cm (½ inch) thick. Spread with 4 tablespoons tomato purée mixed with a little chopped garlic. Then add (per pizza) 4 tablespoons chopped tomatoes, 125g (4 oz) grated mozzarella cheese, 1 teaspoon basil and some black olives. Sprinkle with salt and olive oil, leave for 20 minutes to rise, then bake in a preheated oven, 230°C (450°F) gas mark 8, for 15 minutes. Eat hot. Each pizza should serve two.

Soda Bread

MAKES 2 LARGE LOAVES
750g (1½ lb) white or wholemeal flour
1 teaspoon salt
1 tablespoon cooking oil
2 teaspoons baking powder
1 teaspoon bicarbonate of soda
300ml (½ pint) warm water
150g (5 oz) yoghurt

Mix all the ingredients together in a large bowl, adding a little more flour if the mixture is too soft. Shape into 2 large round loaves and place on a baking sheet. Make a cut across the top and bake in a preheated oven, 220°C (425°F) gas mark 7, for 25–30 minutes. Eat while still warm if you can.

Index